HAMSA COLORING BOOK

This book belong to:

____

ABOUT THIS BOOK

Thank you for purchasing this quality coloring book from Sunrise Coloring!

Inside this book are 40 unique and fanstatic Hamsa coloring pages designed especially for adult.

Each image is on its own page with a BLANK backside to help avoid color bleed-through if you color with markers or other ink based pens.

If you use something other than colored pencils or crayons, we also recom-mend placing a sheet of paper or some other blotter between your coloring page and the one beneath it while you work.

We hope you enjoy your Hamsa Coloring Book!

TEST COLOR PAGE

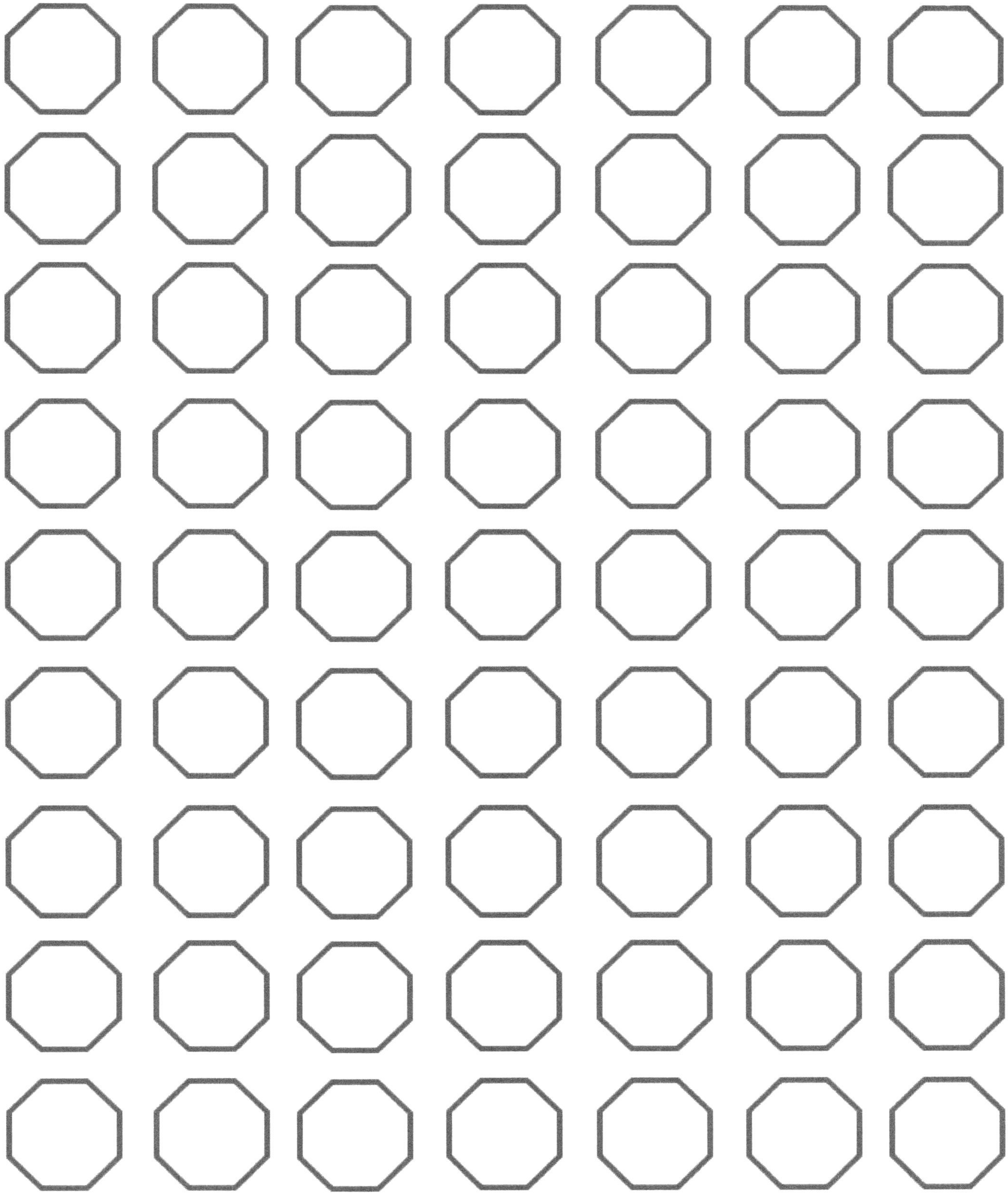

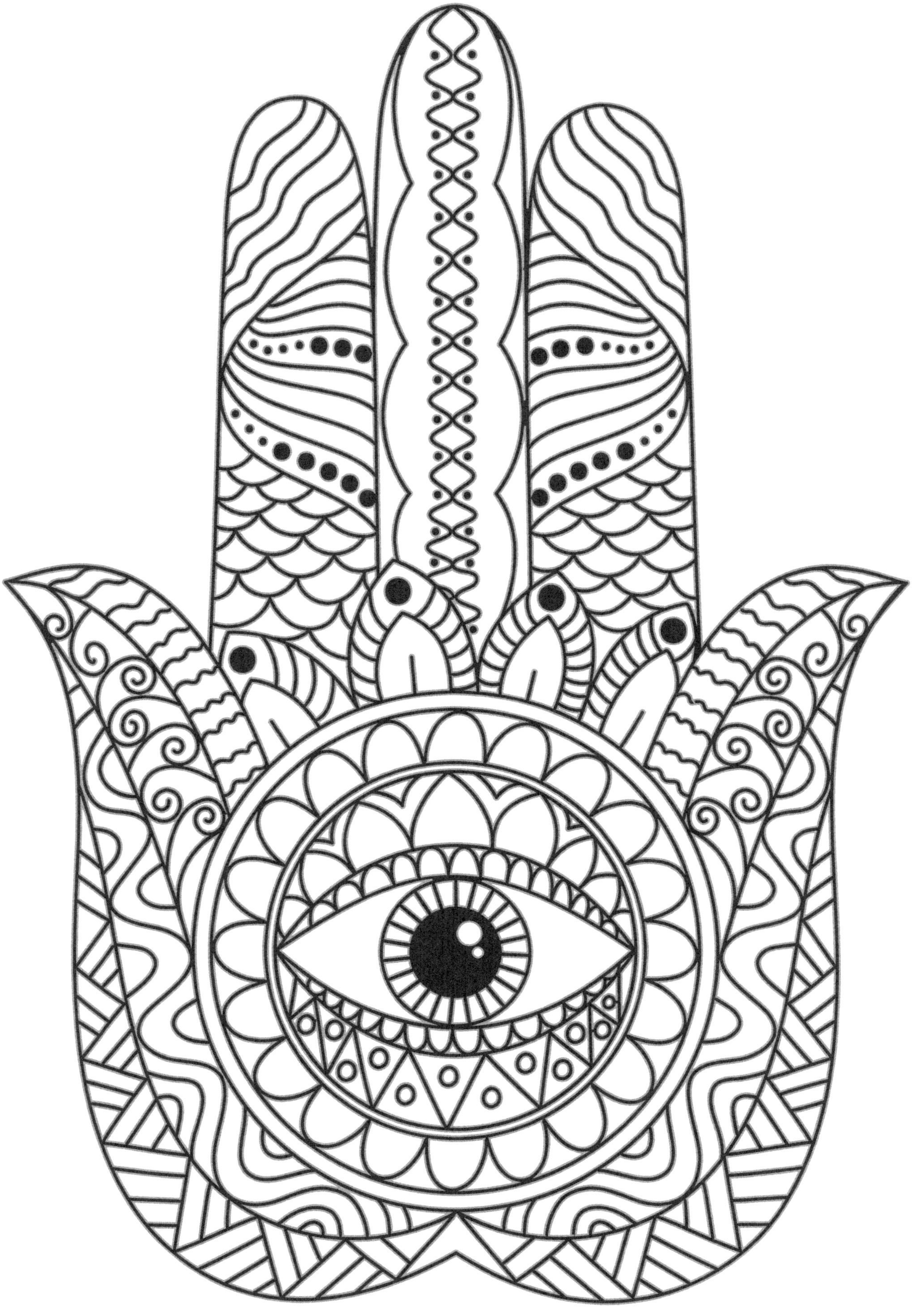

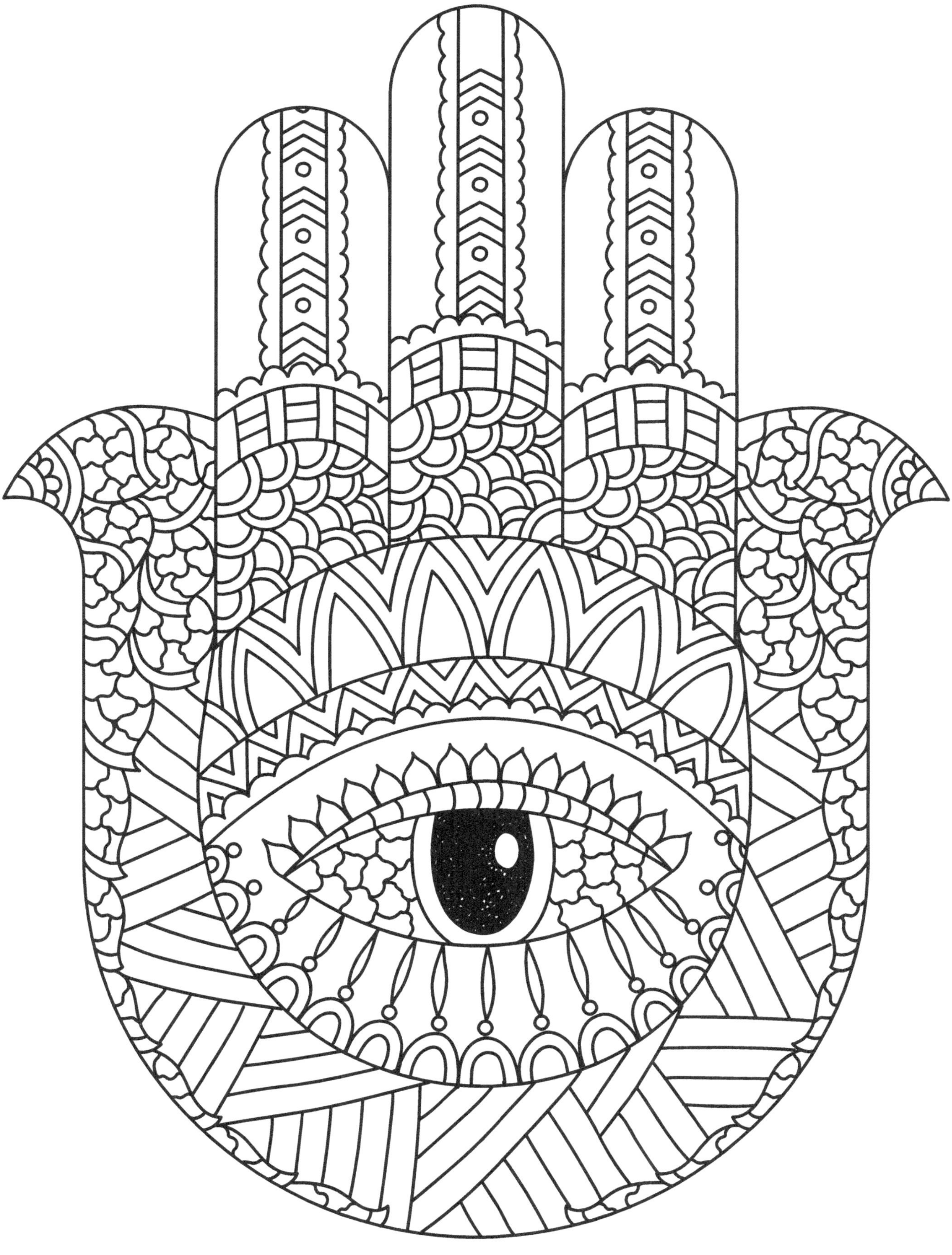

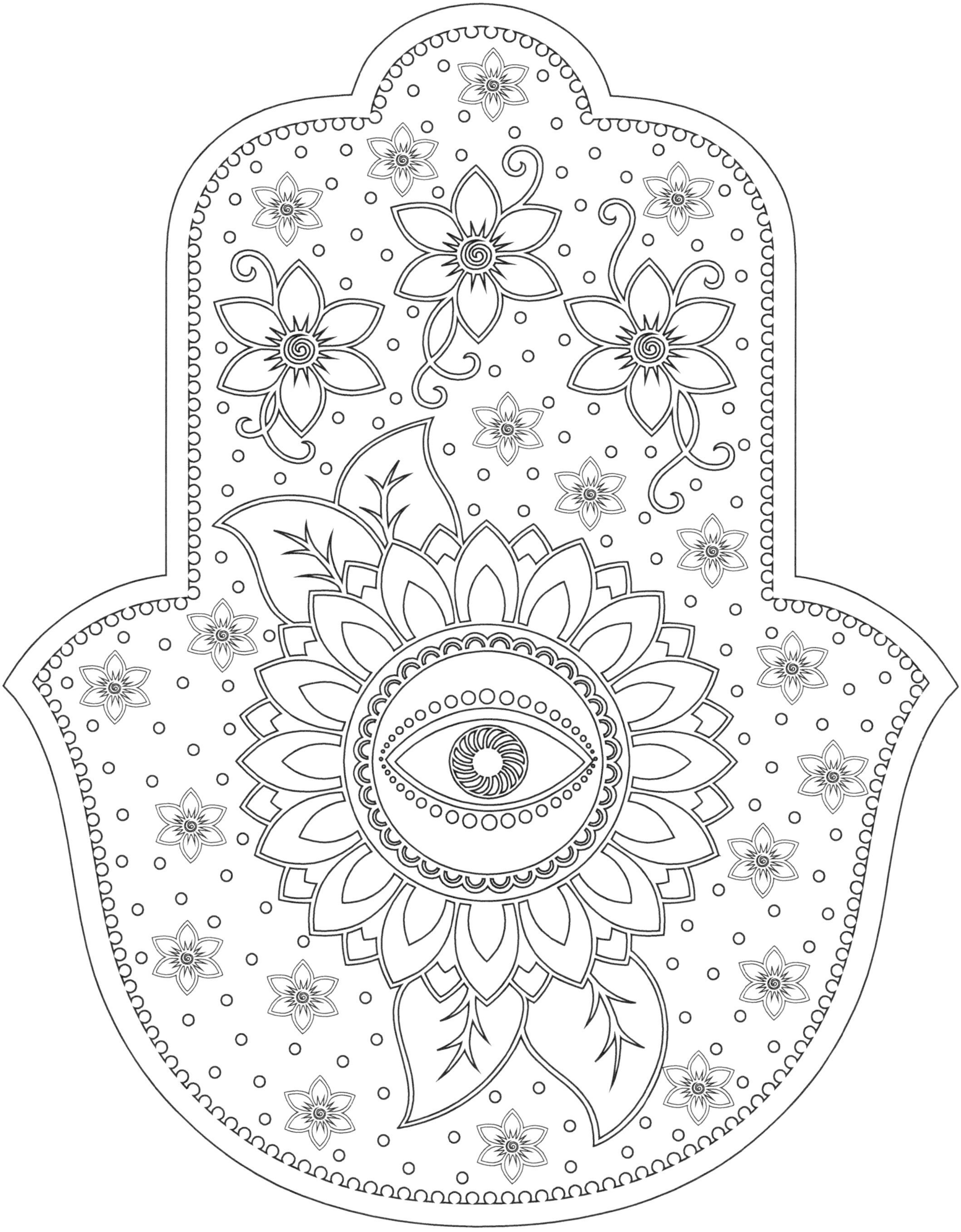

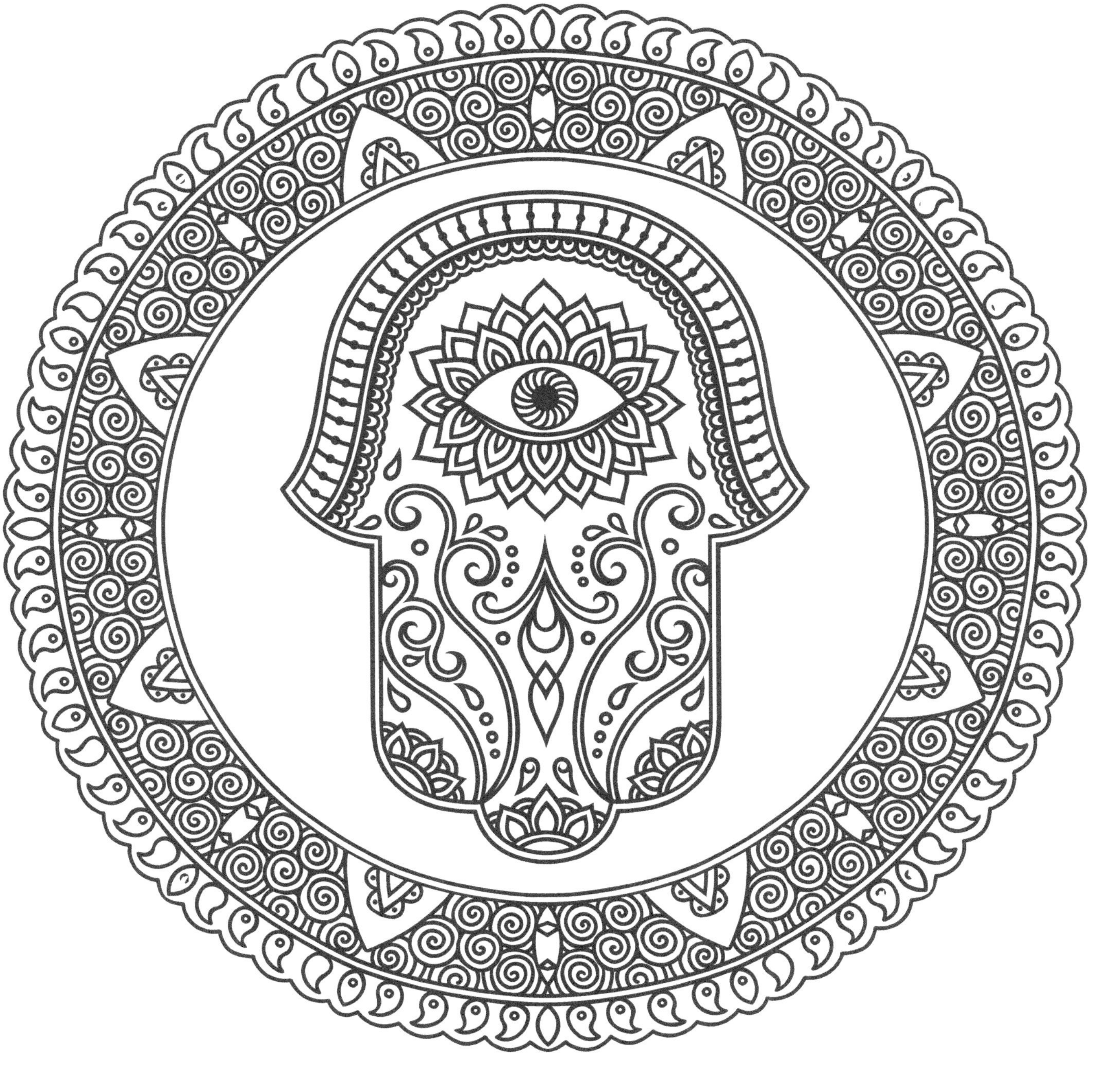

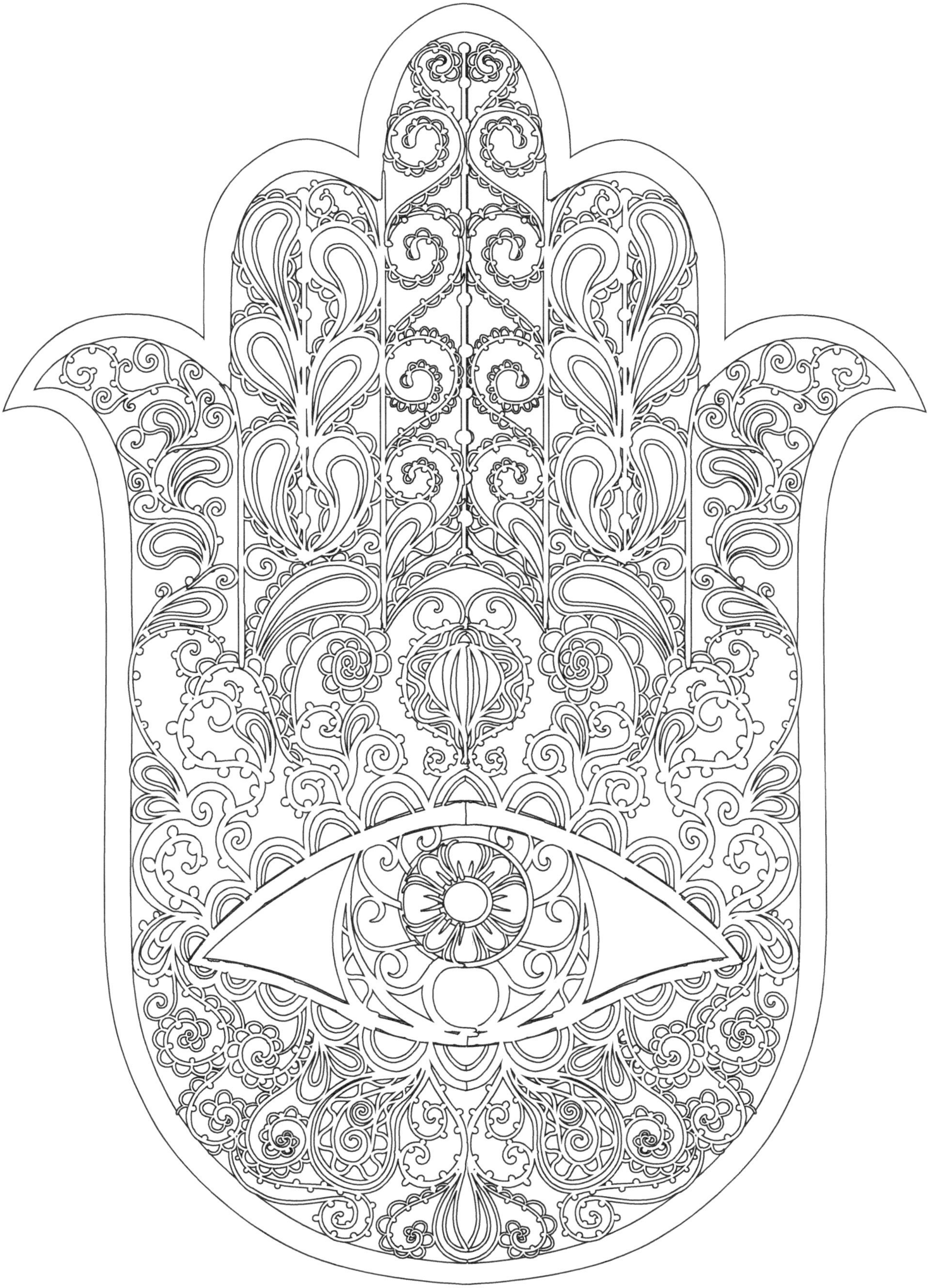

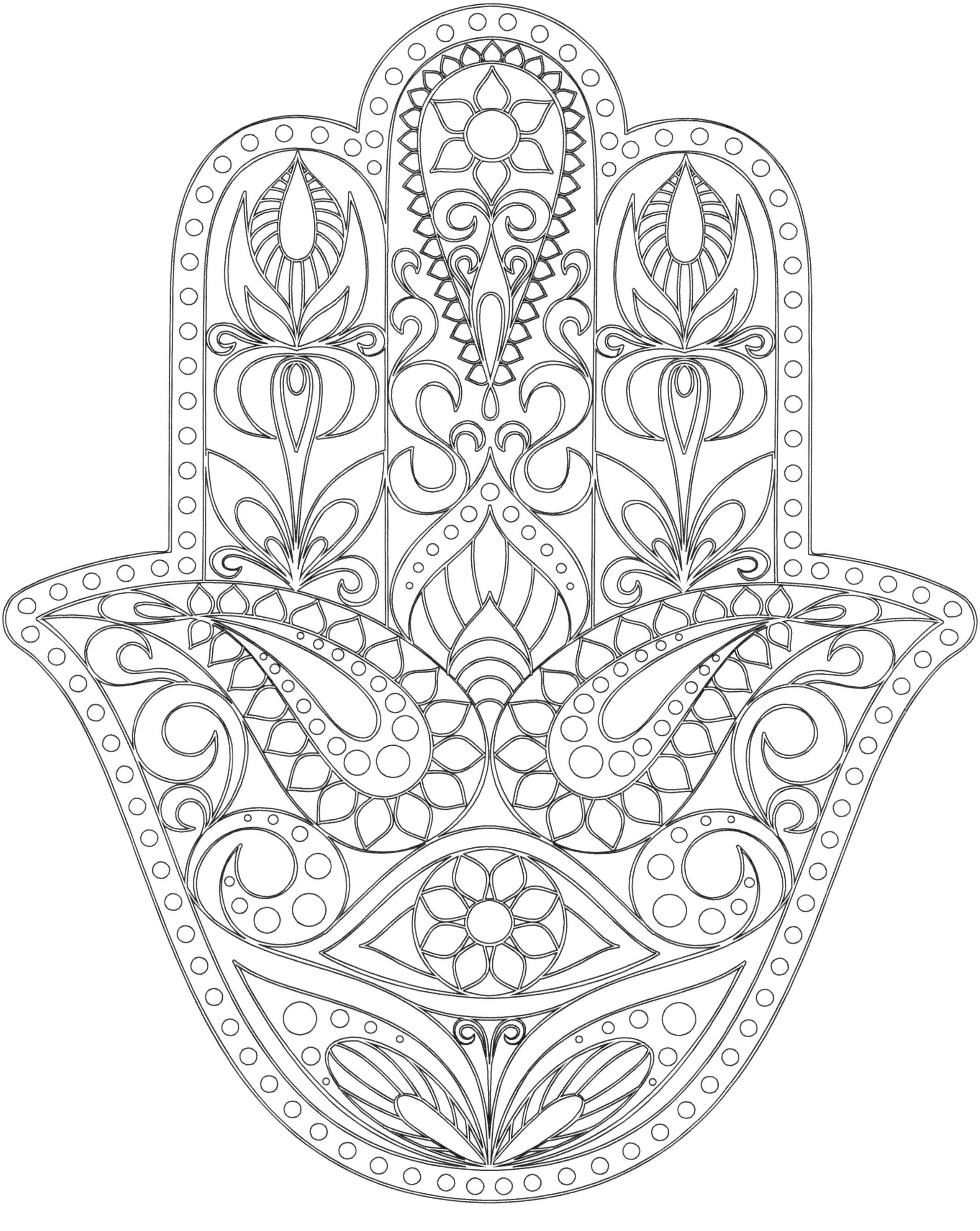

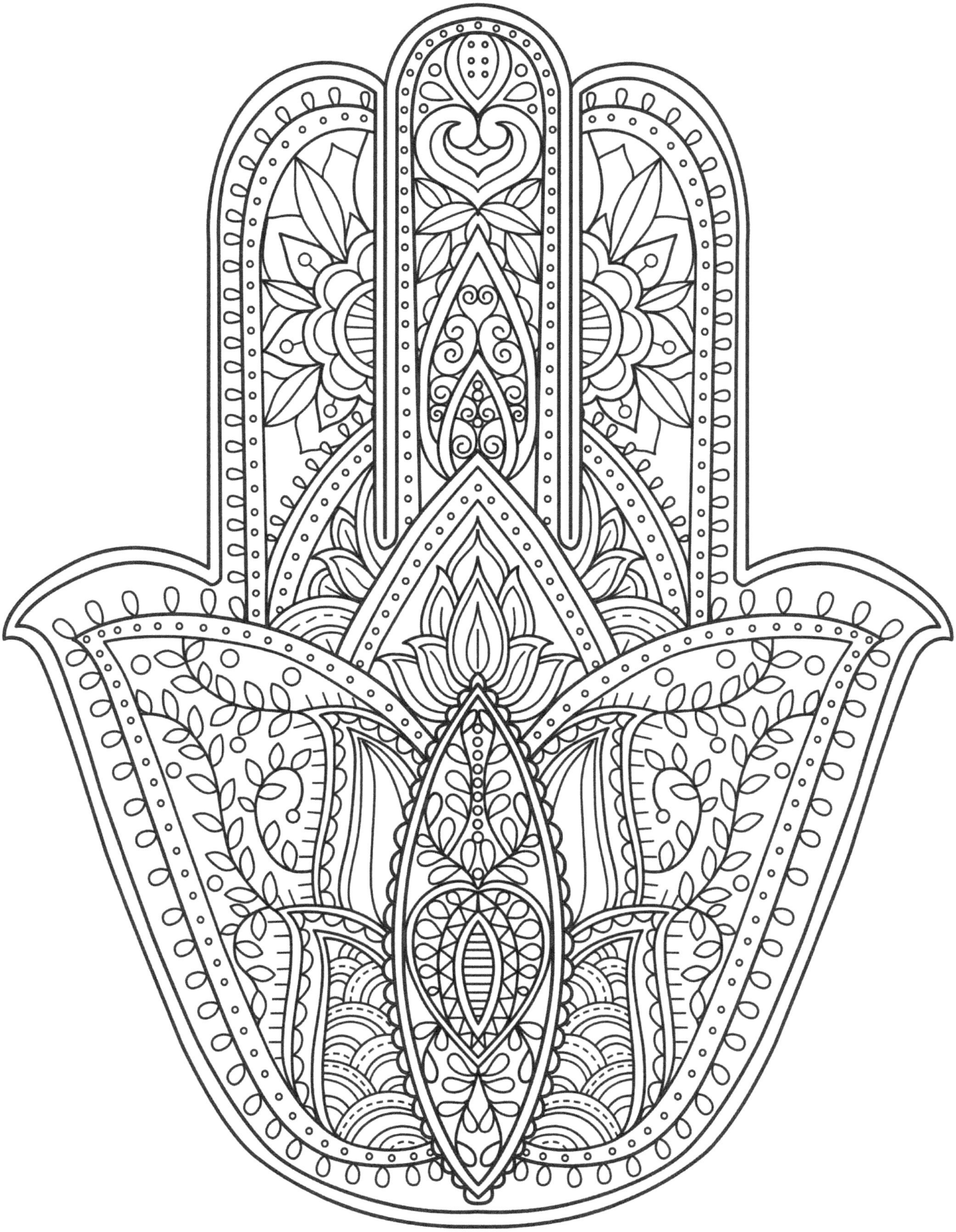

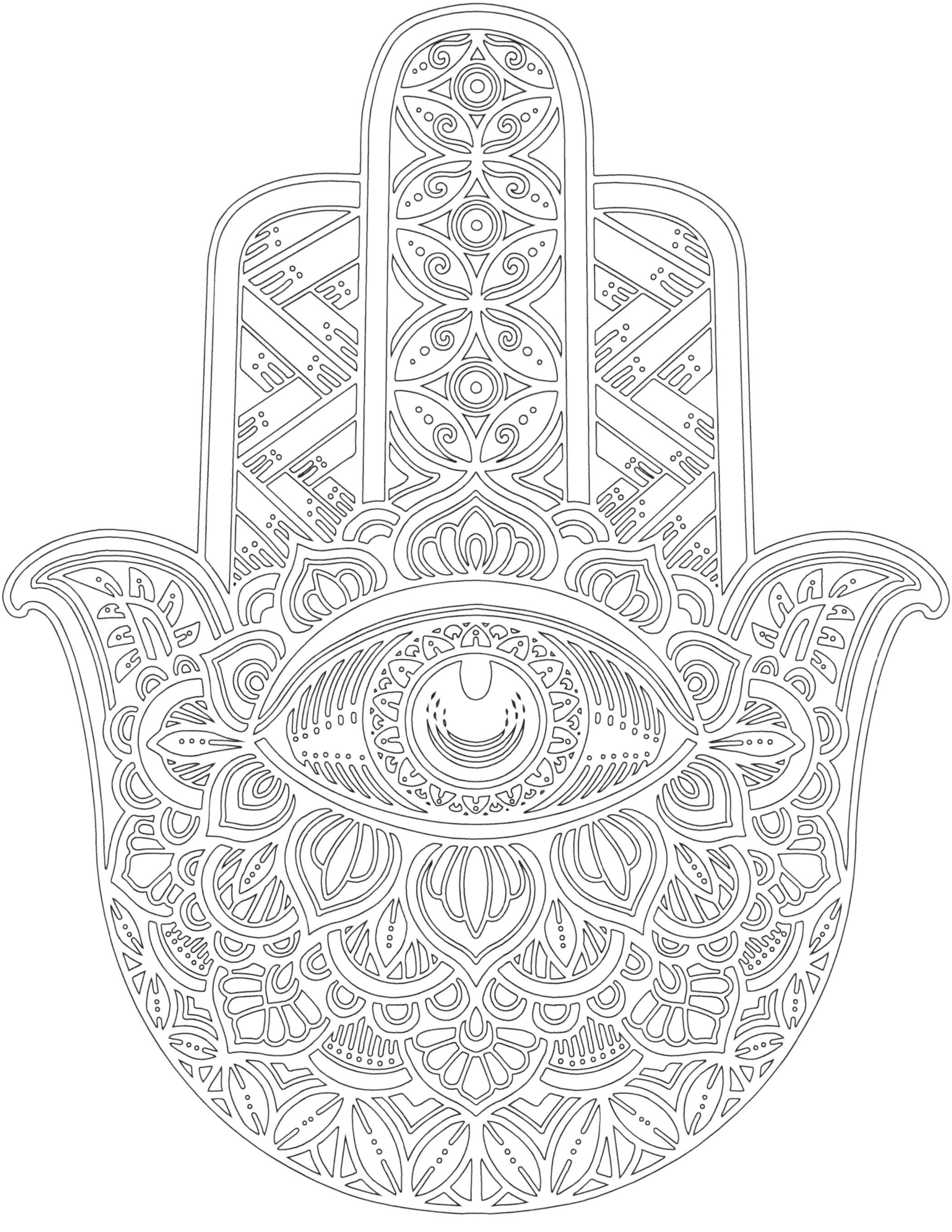

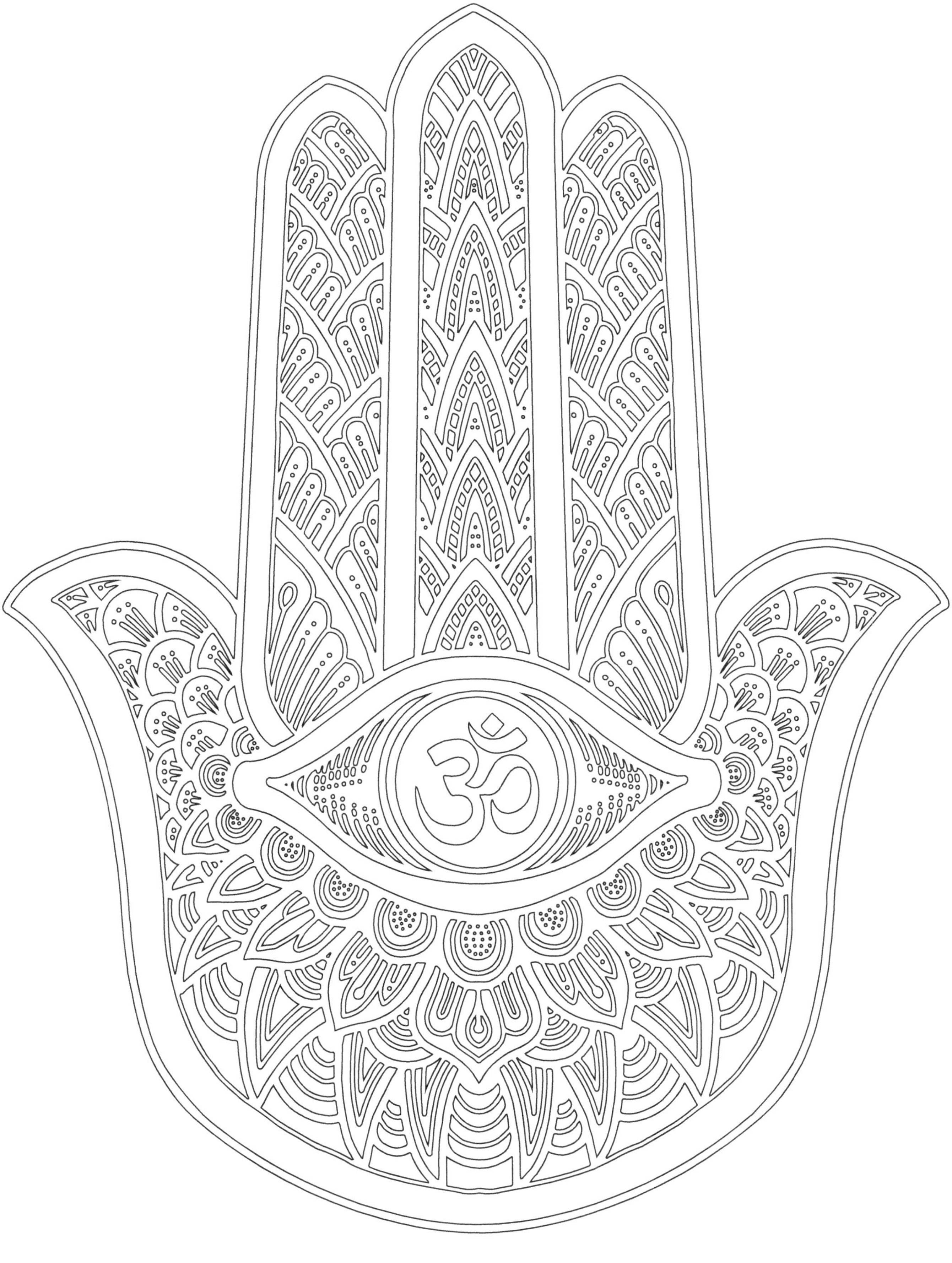

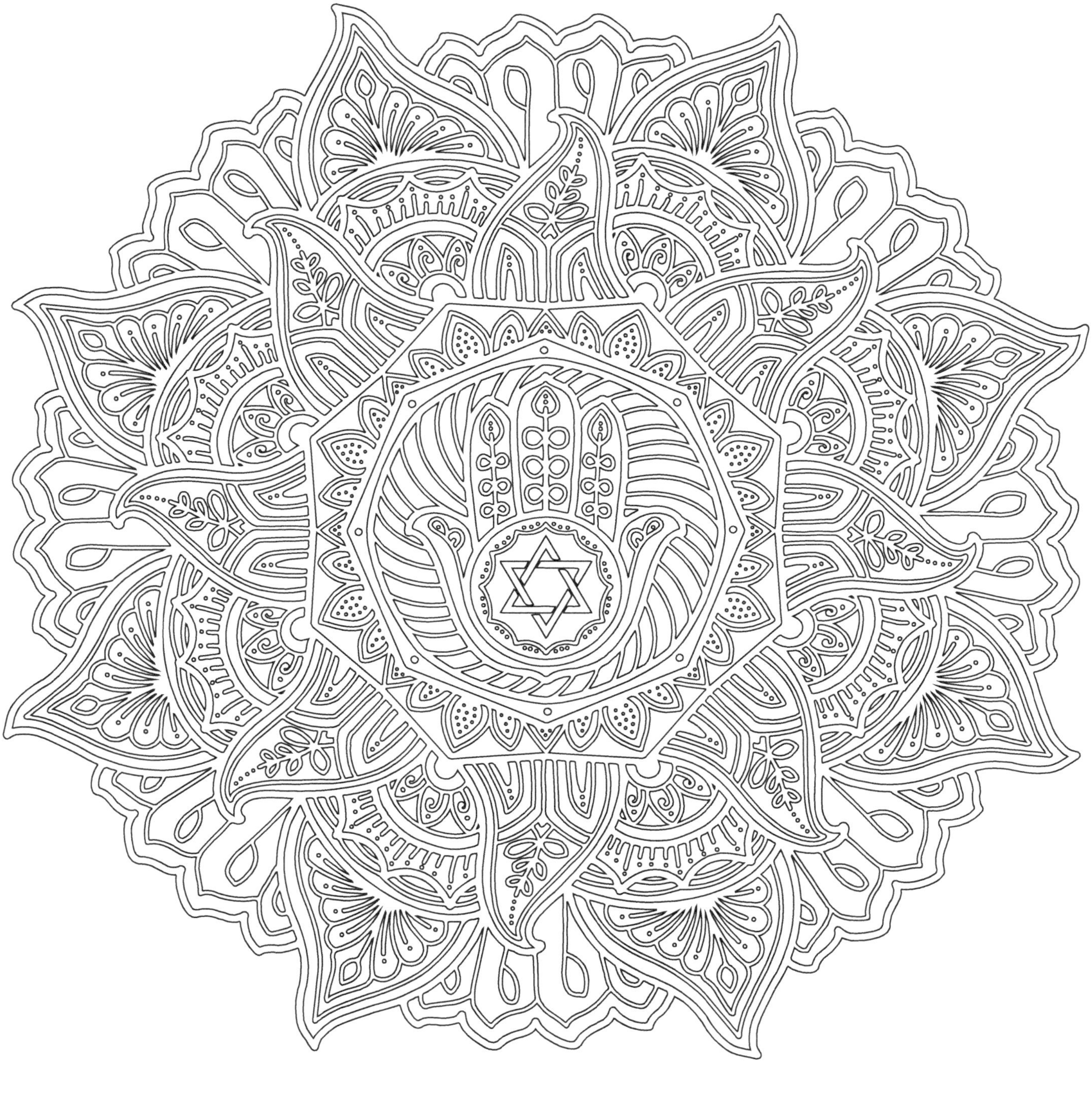

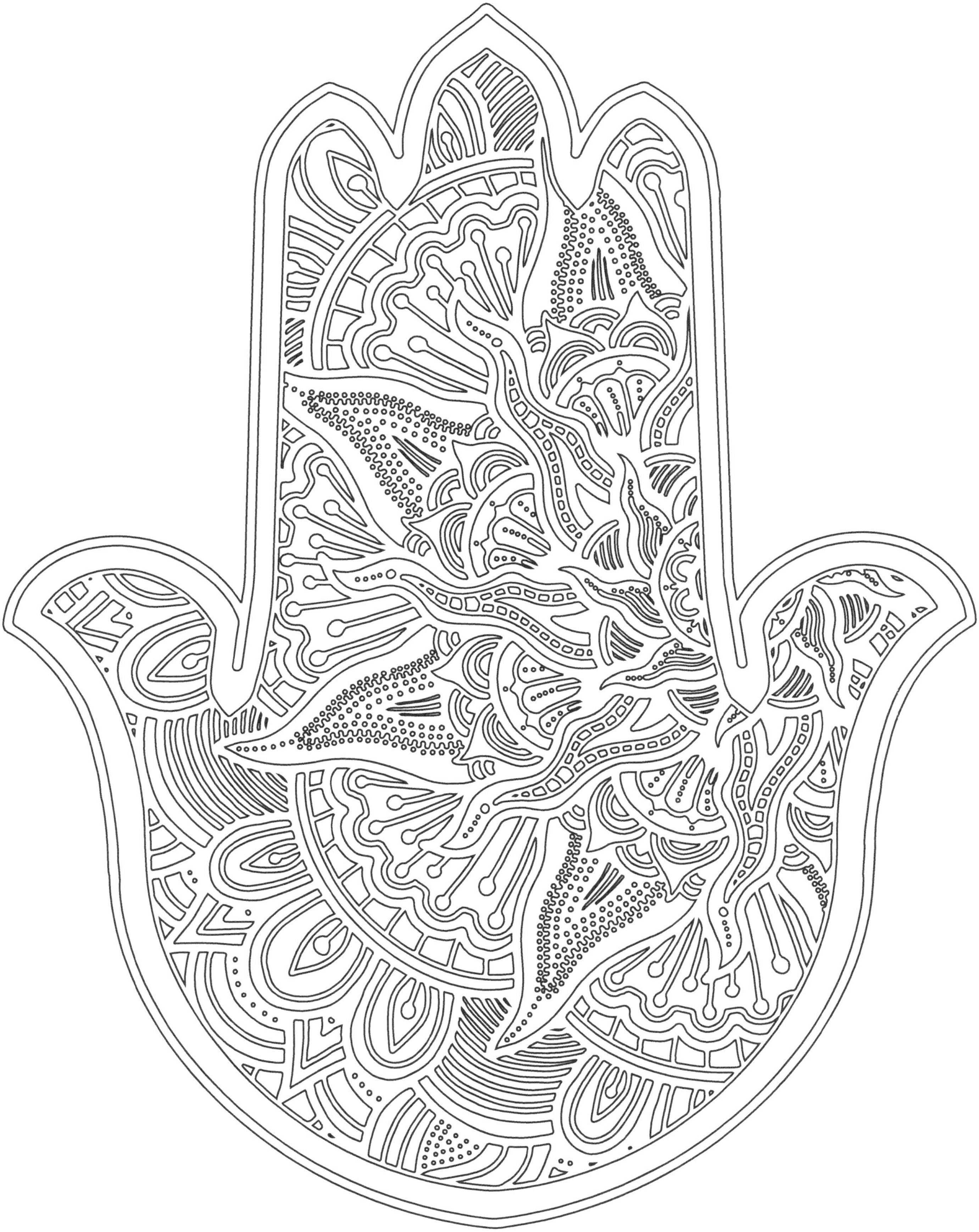

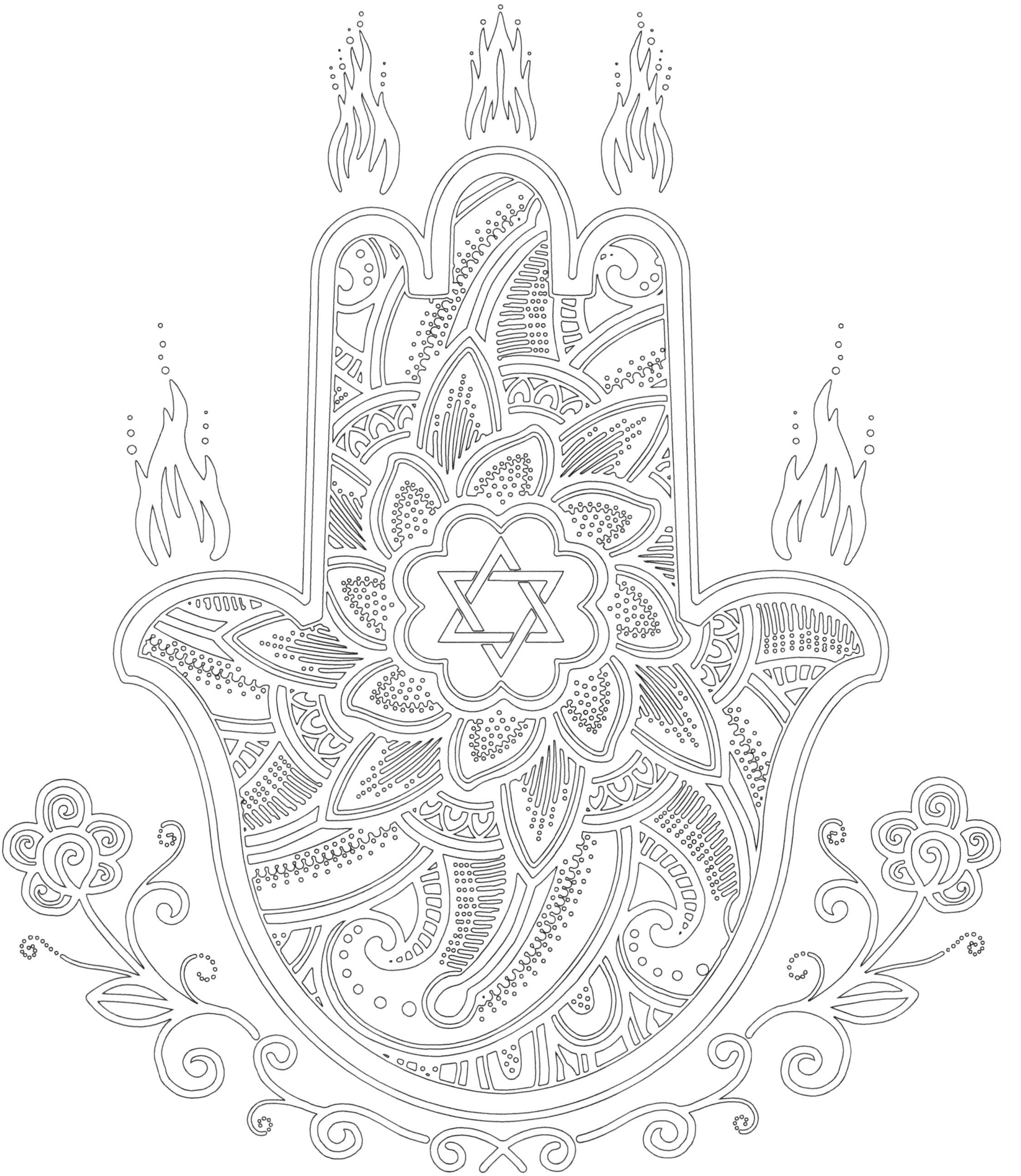

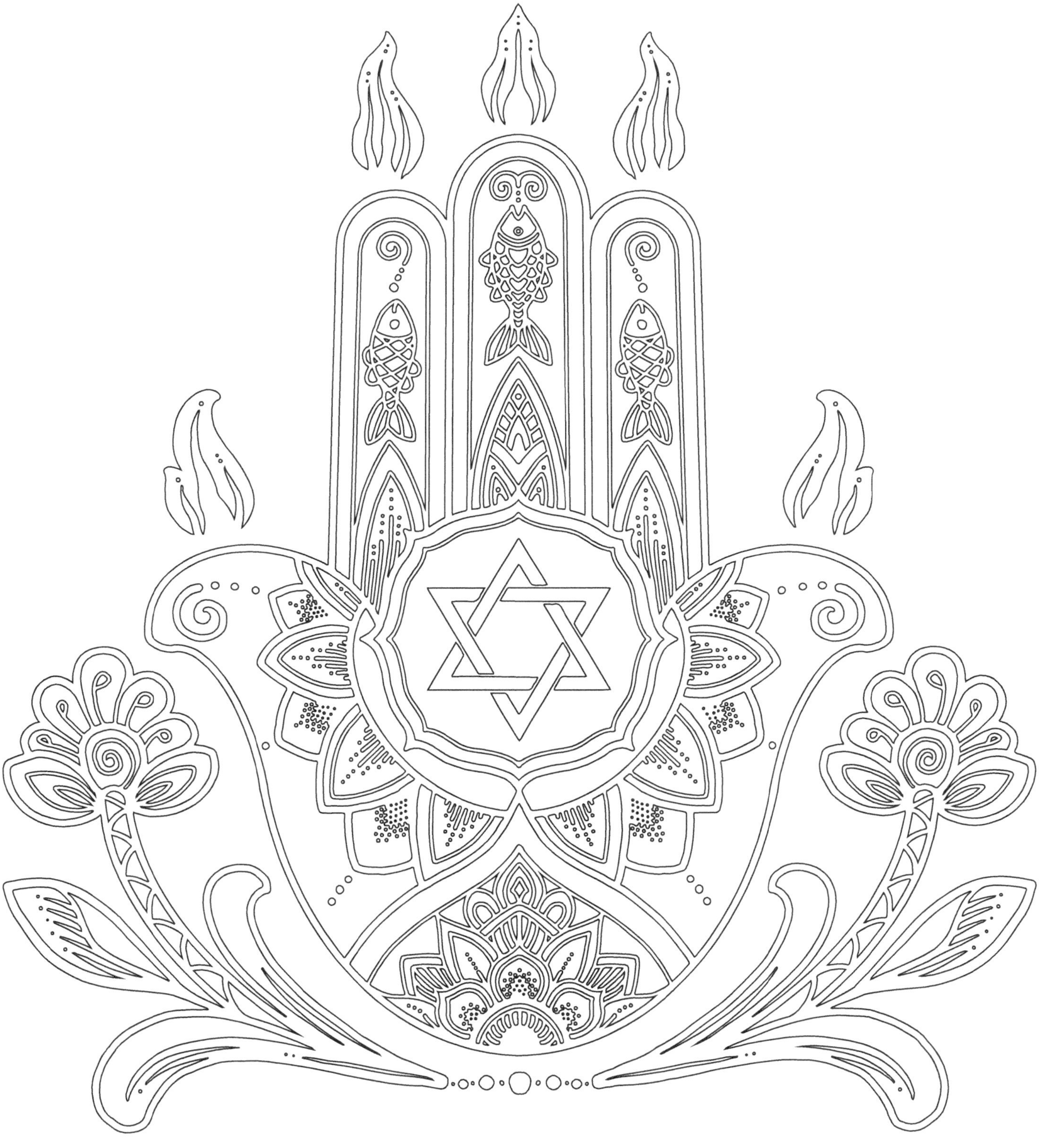

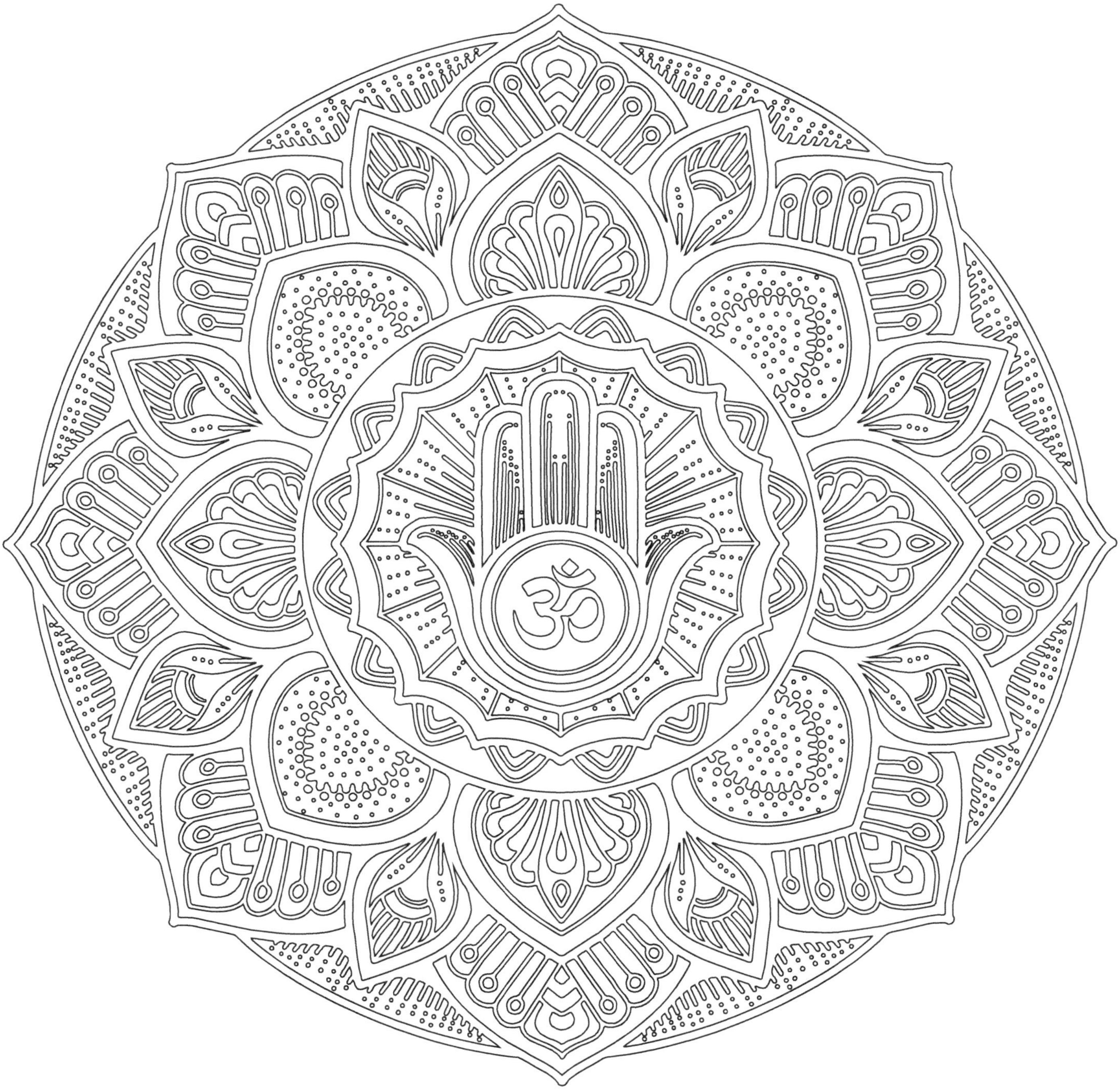

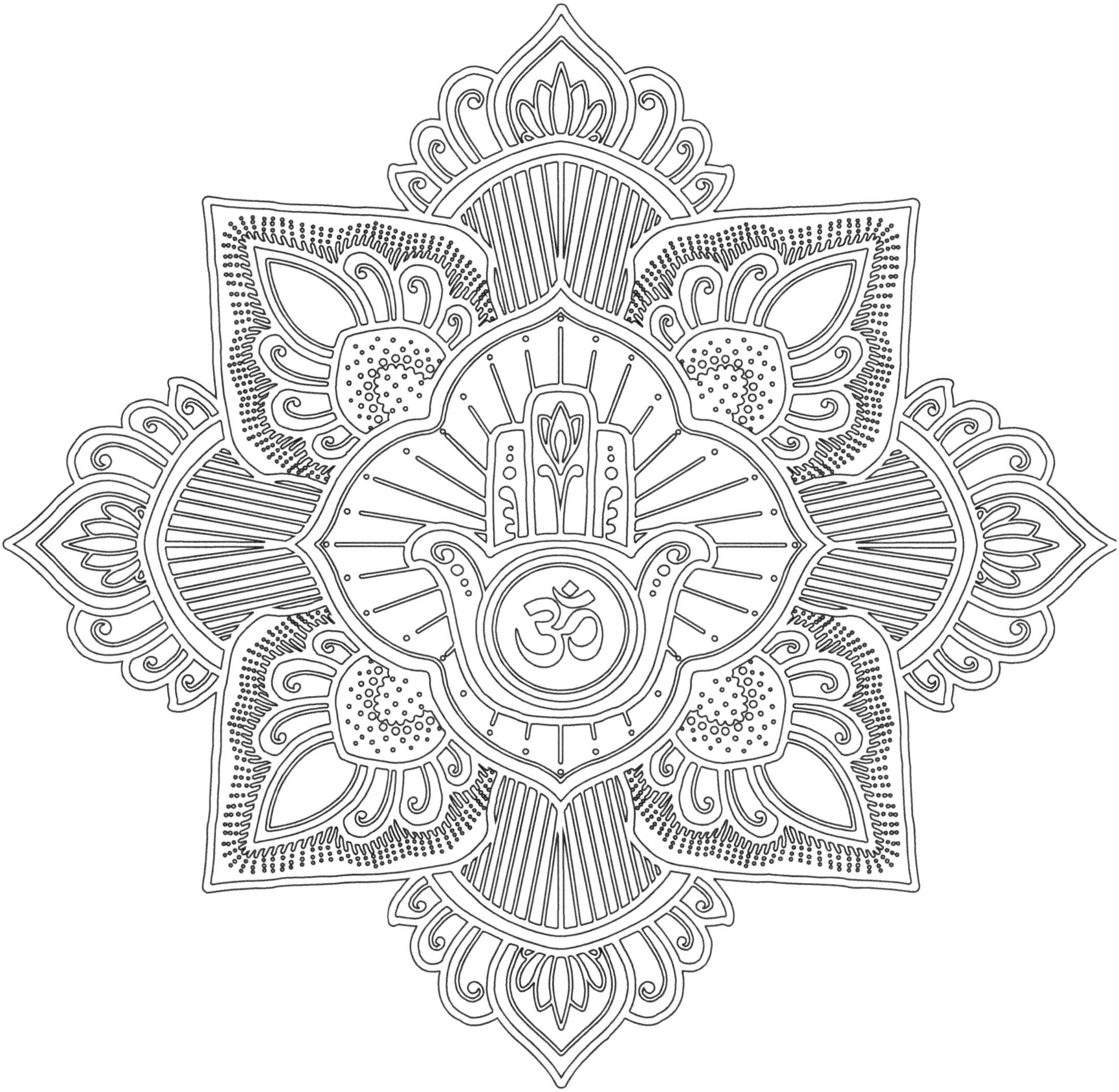

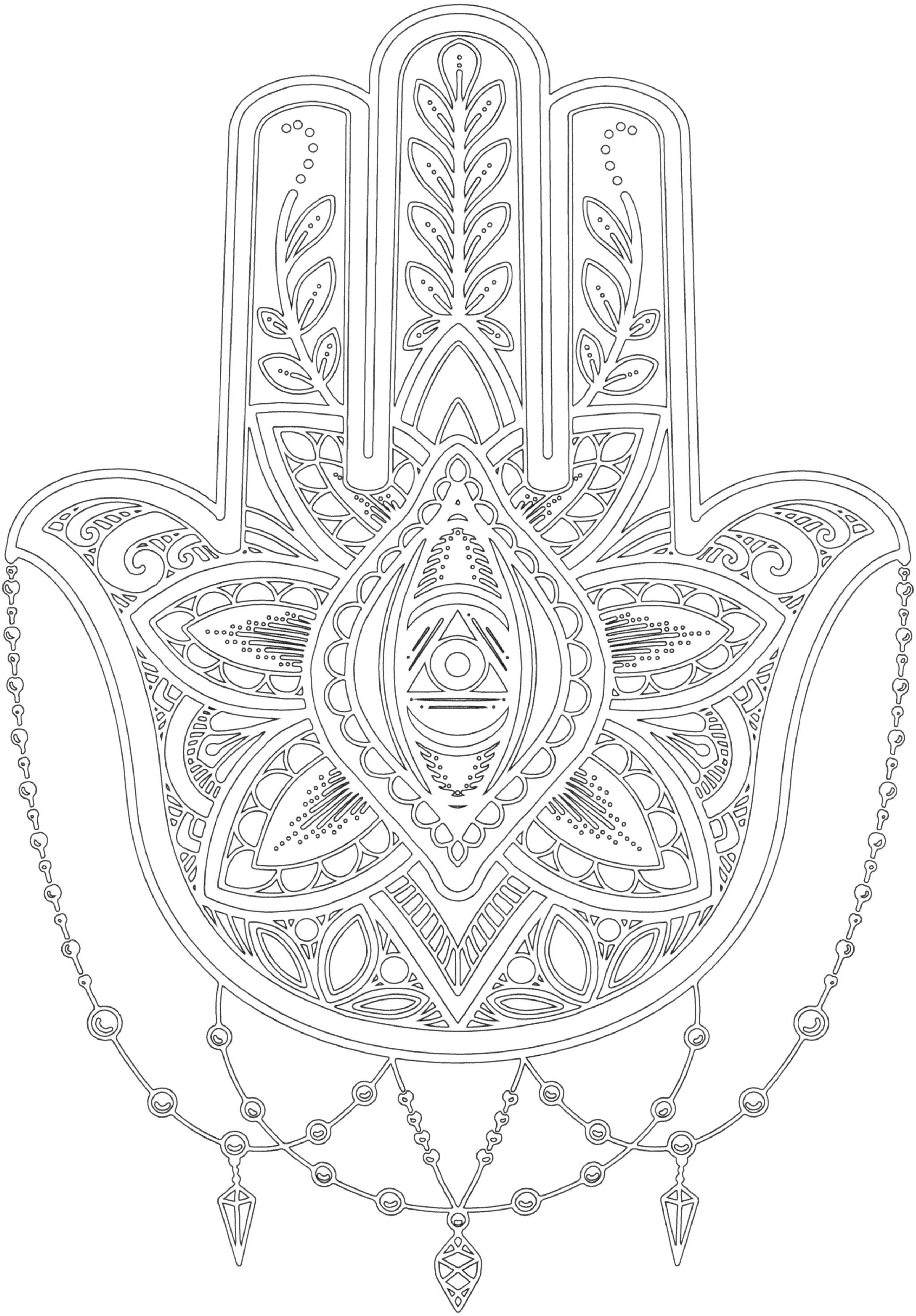

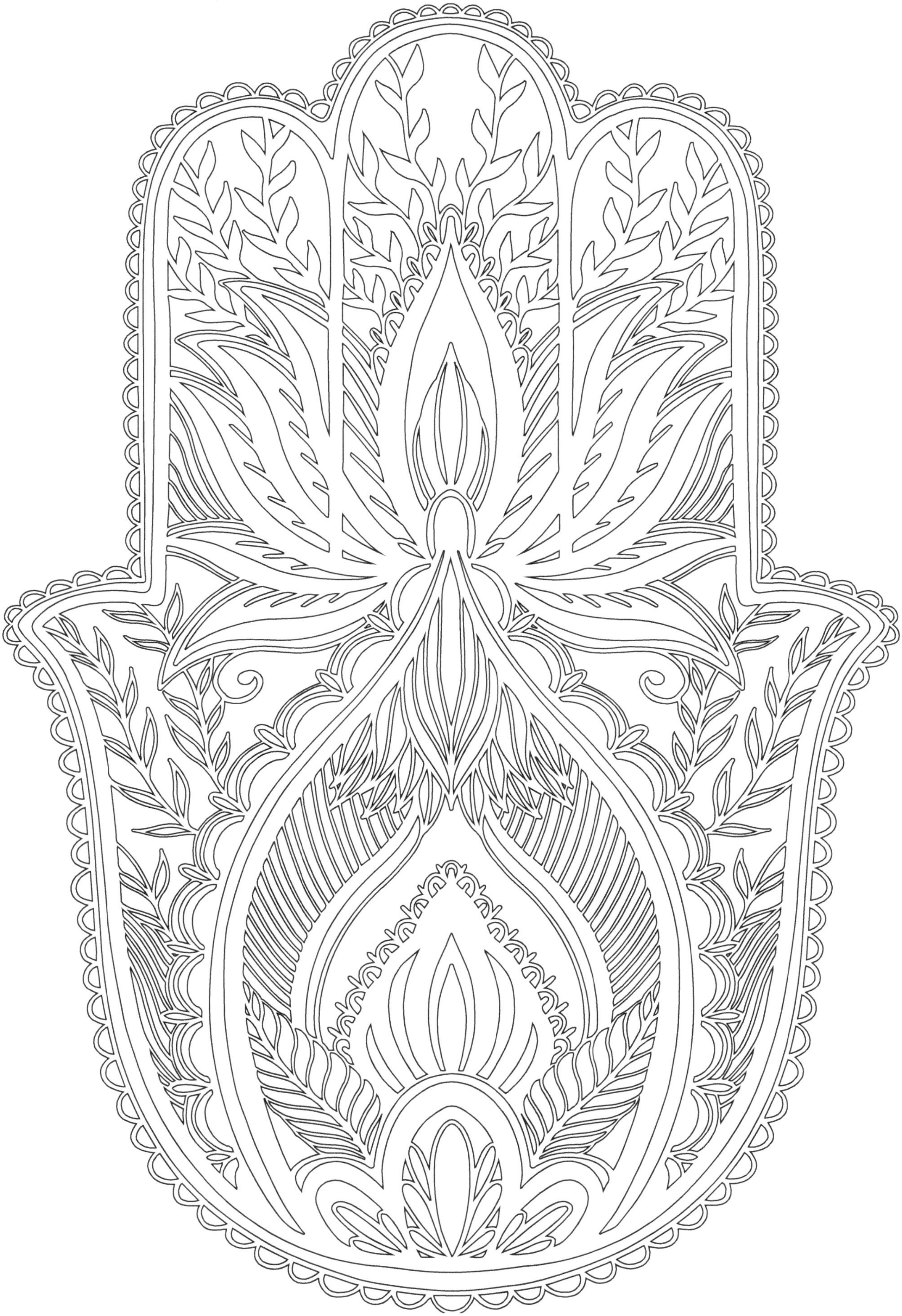

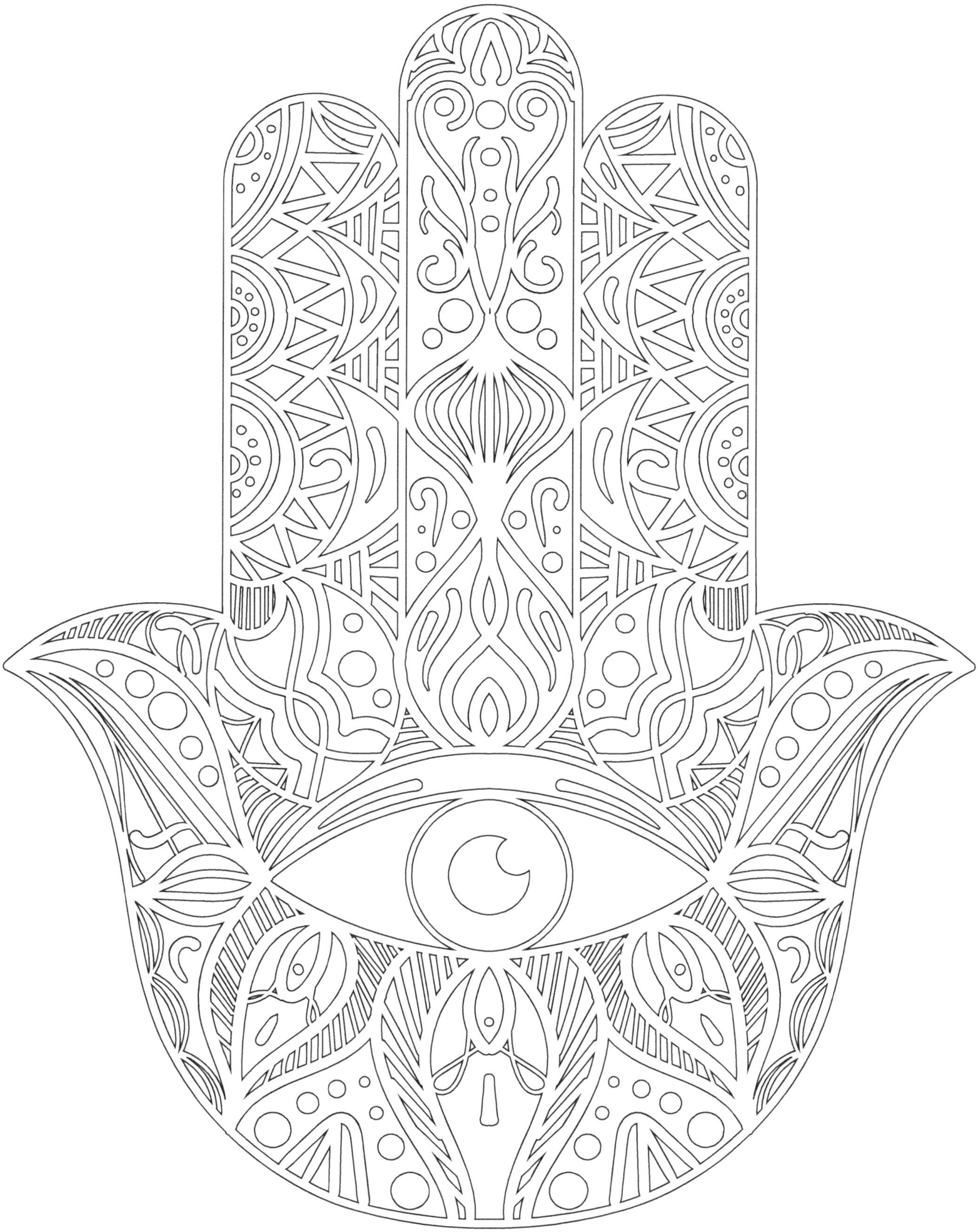

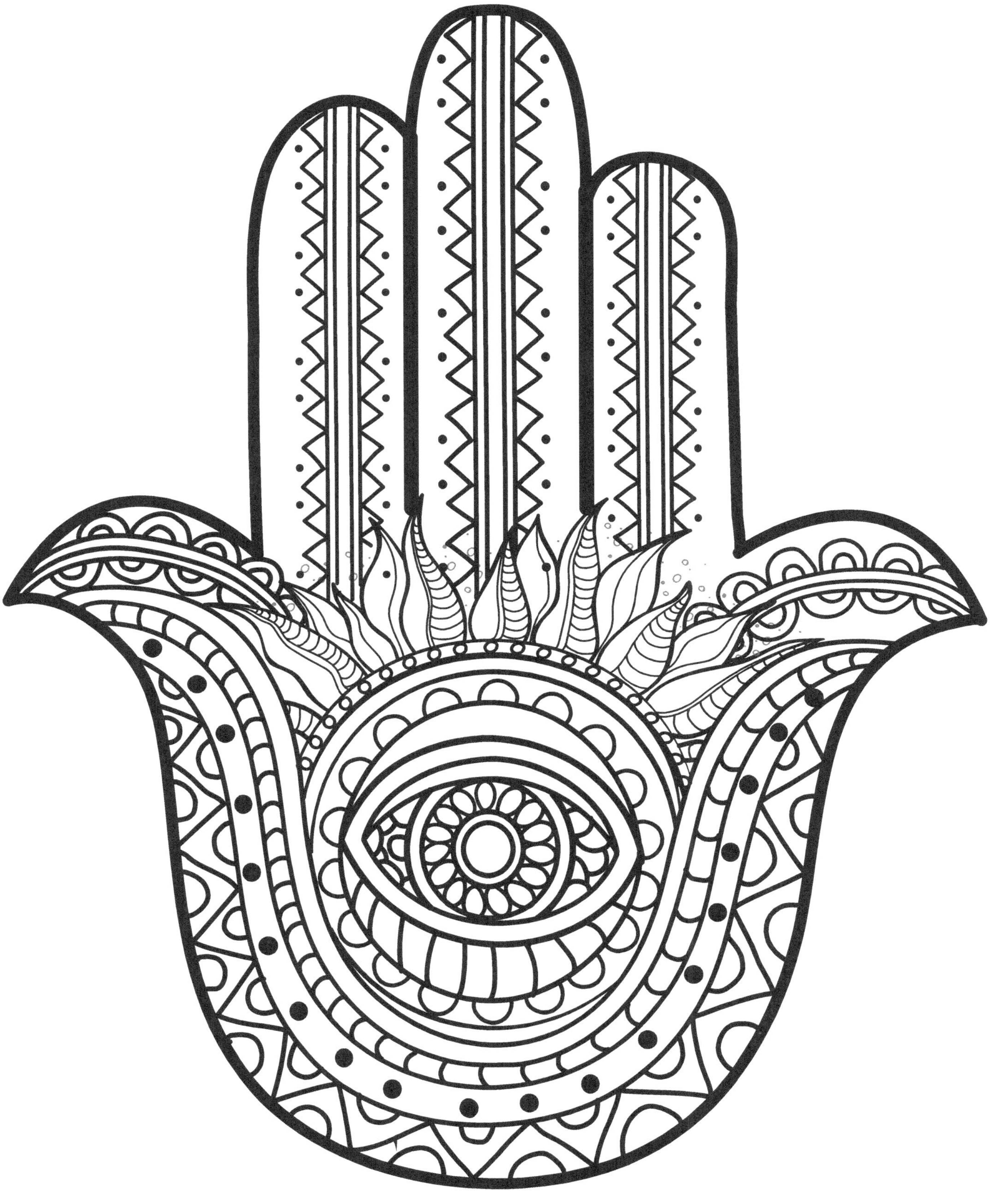

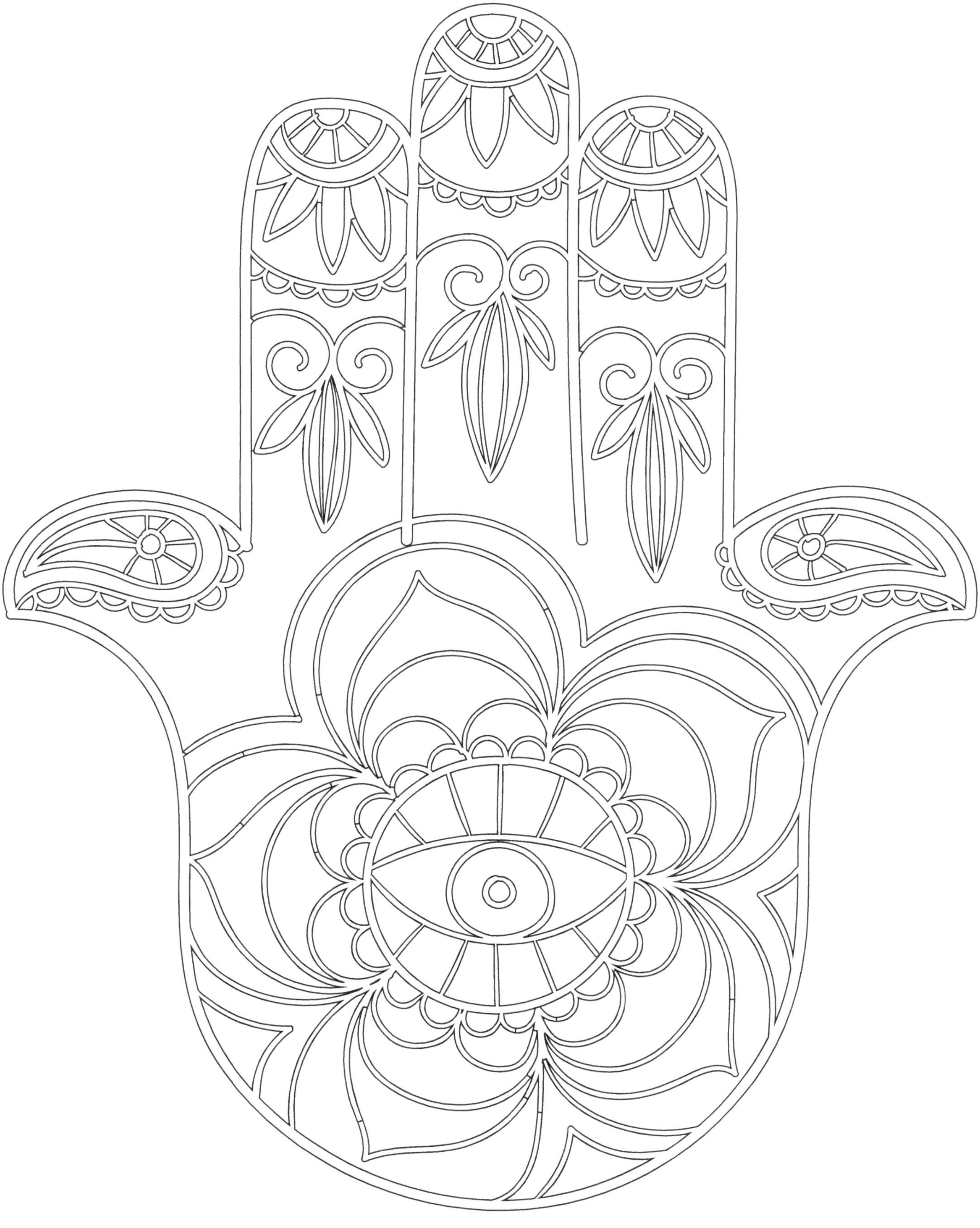

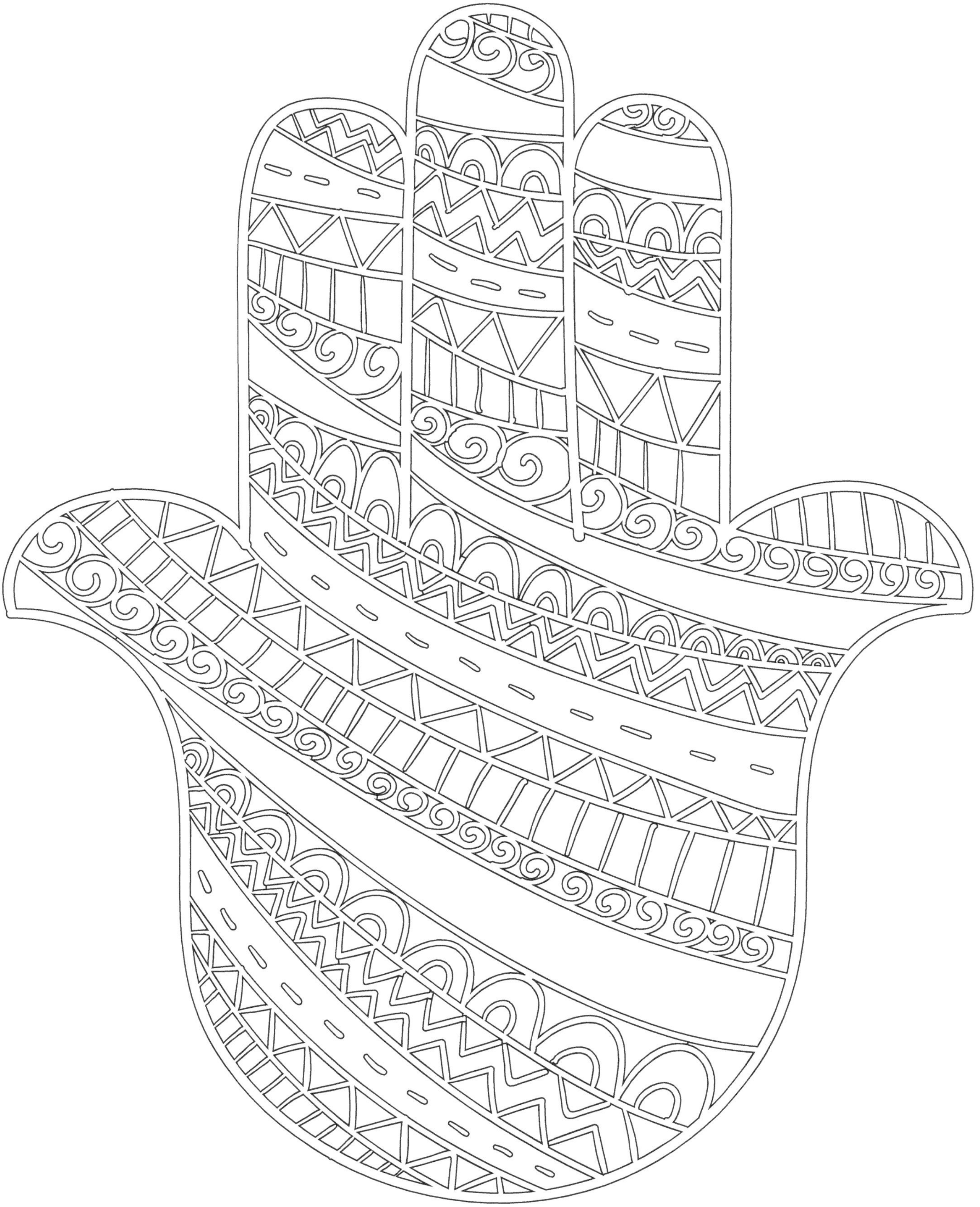

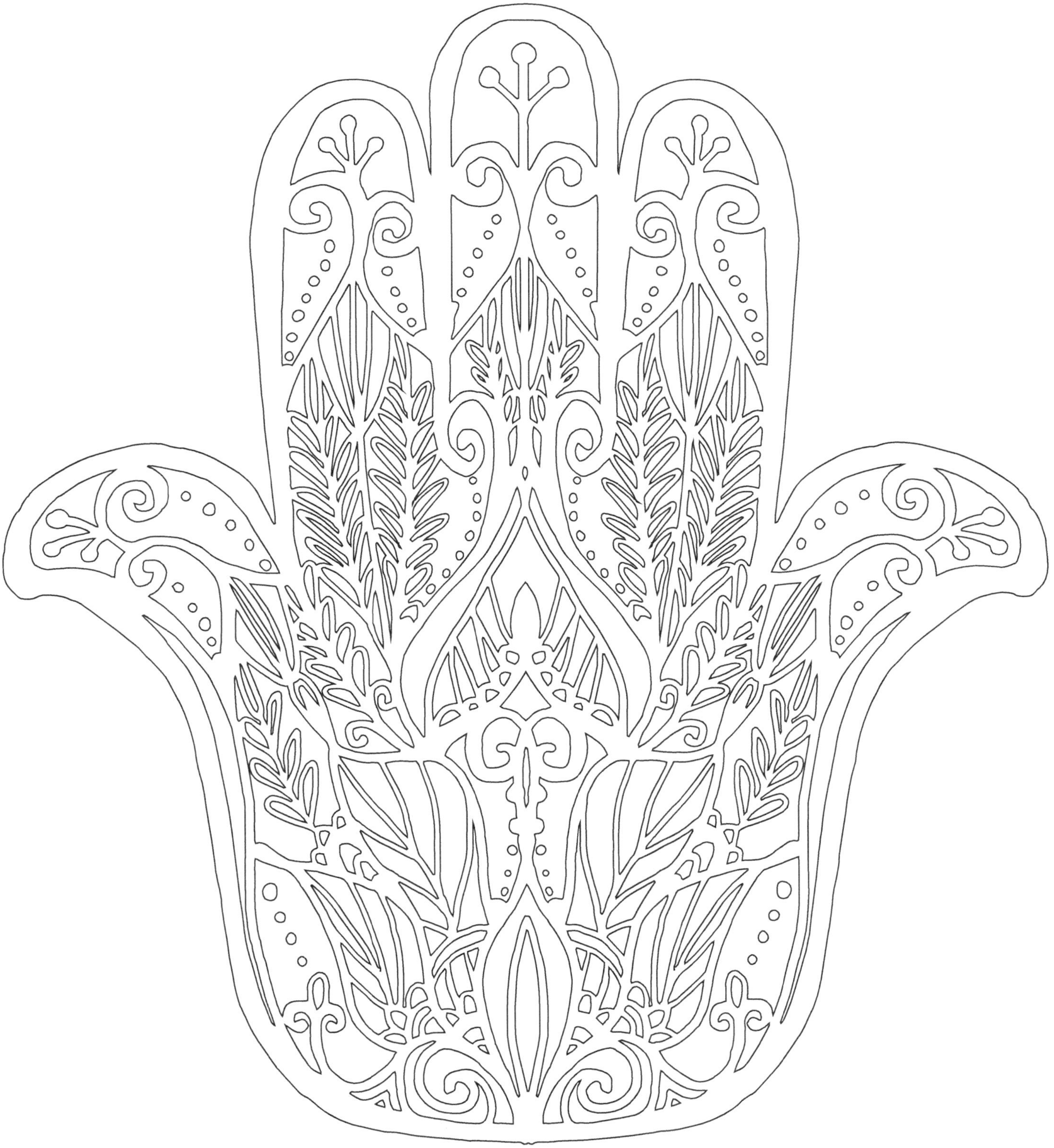

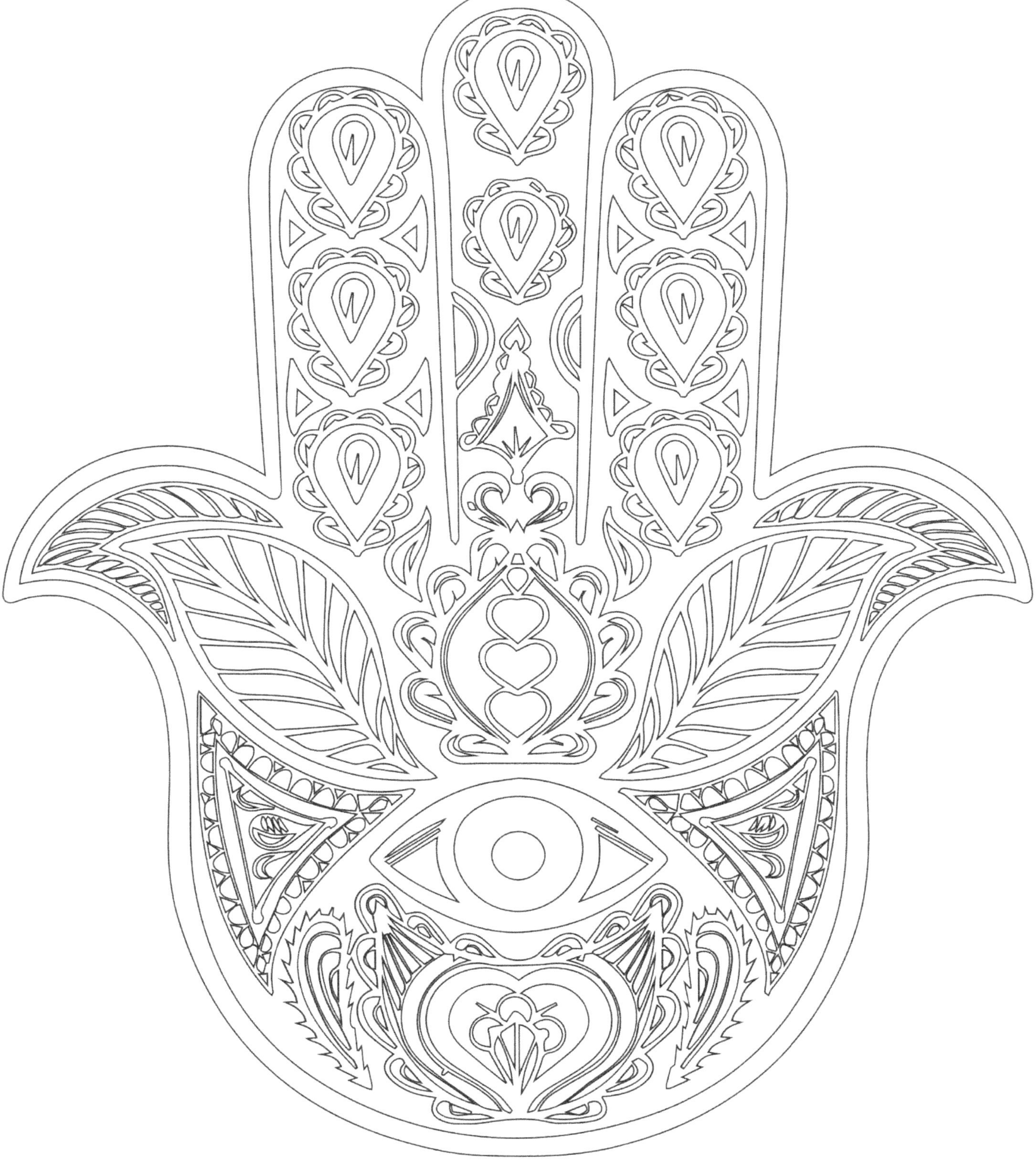

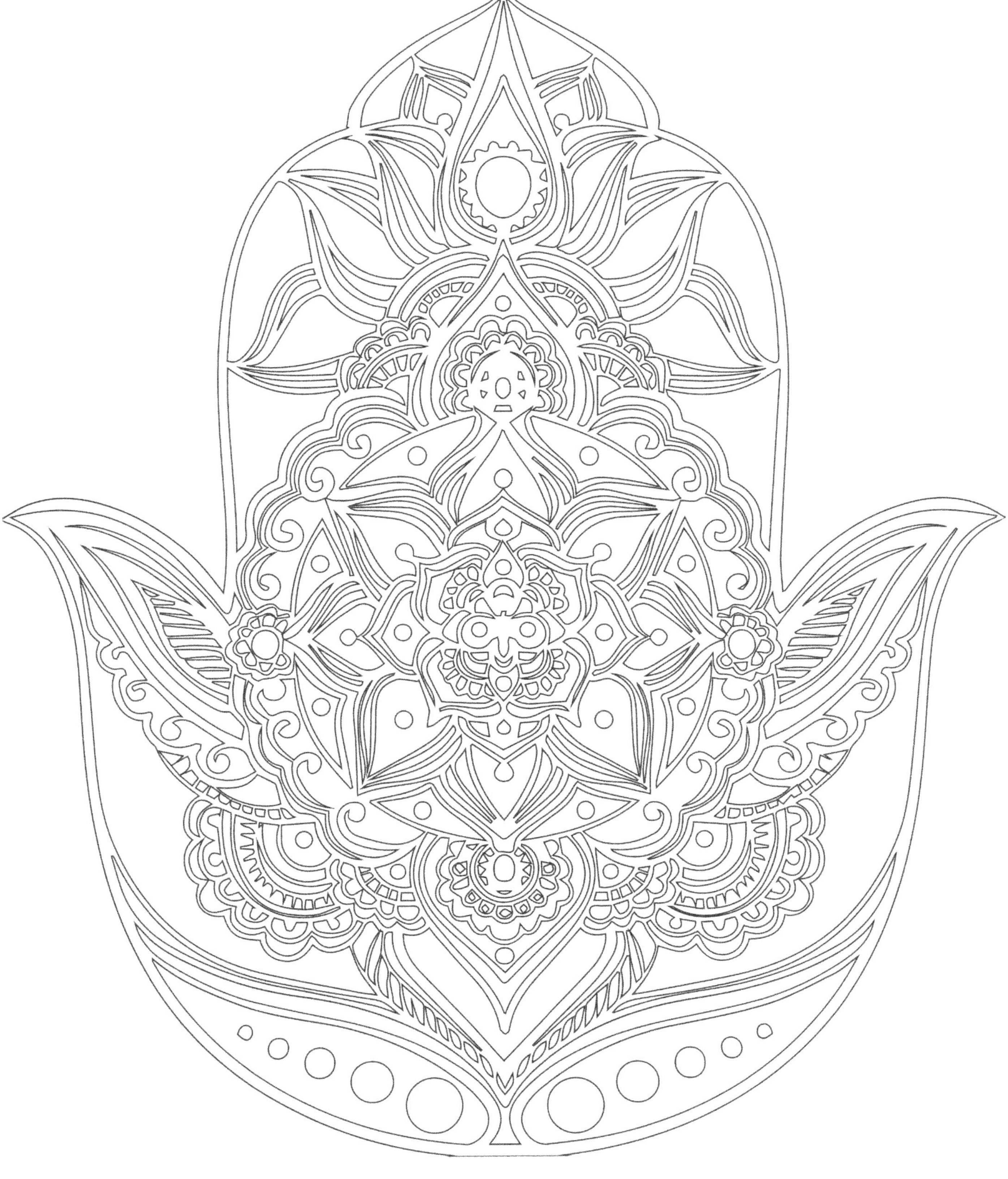

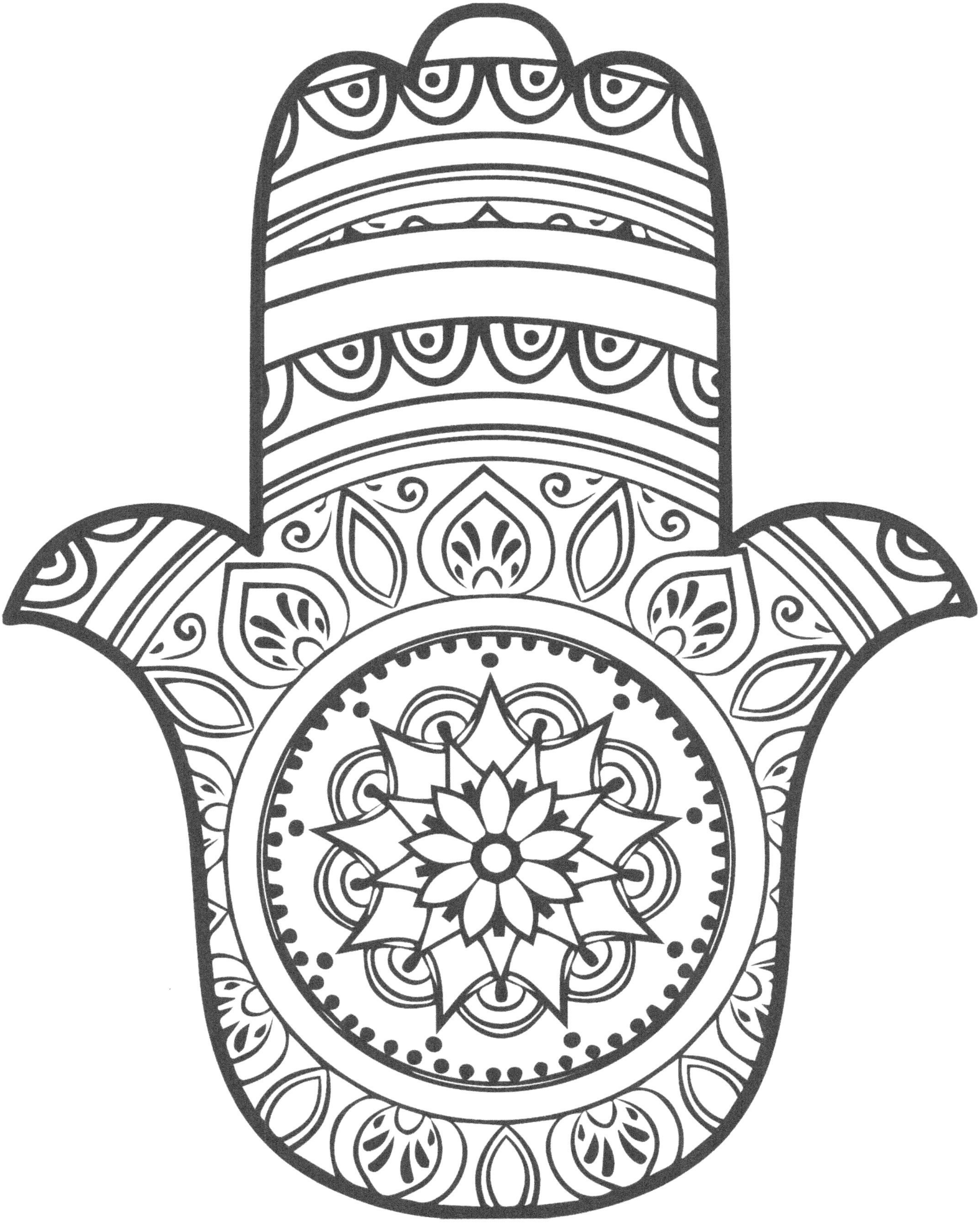

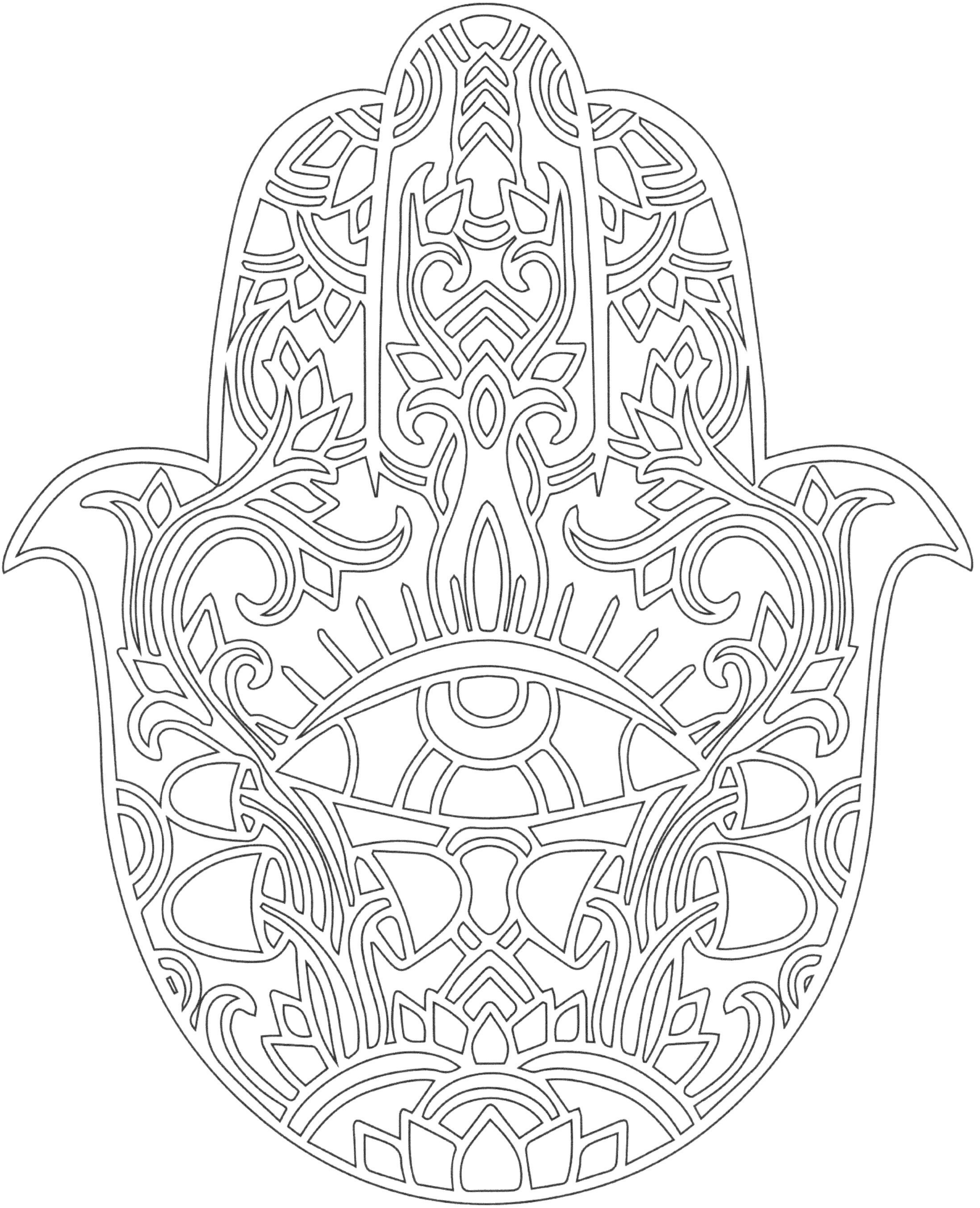

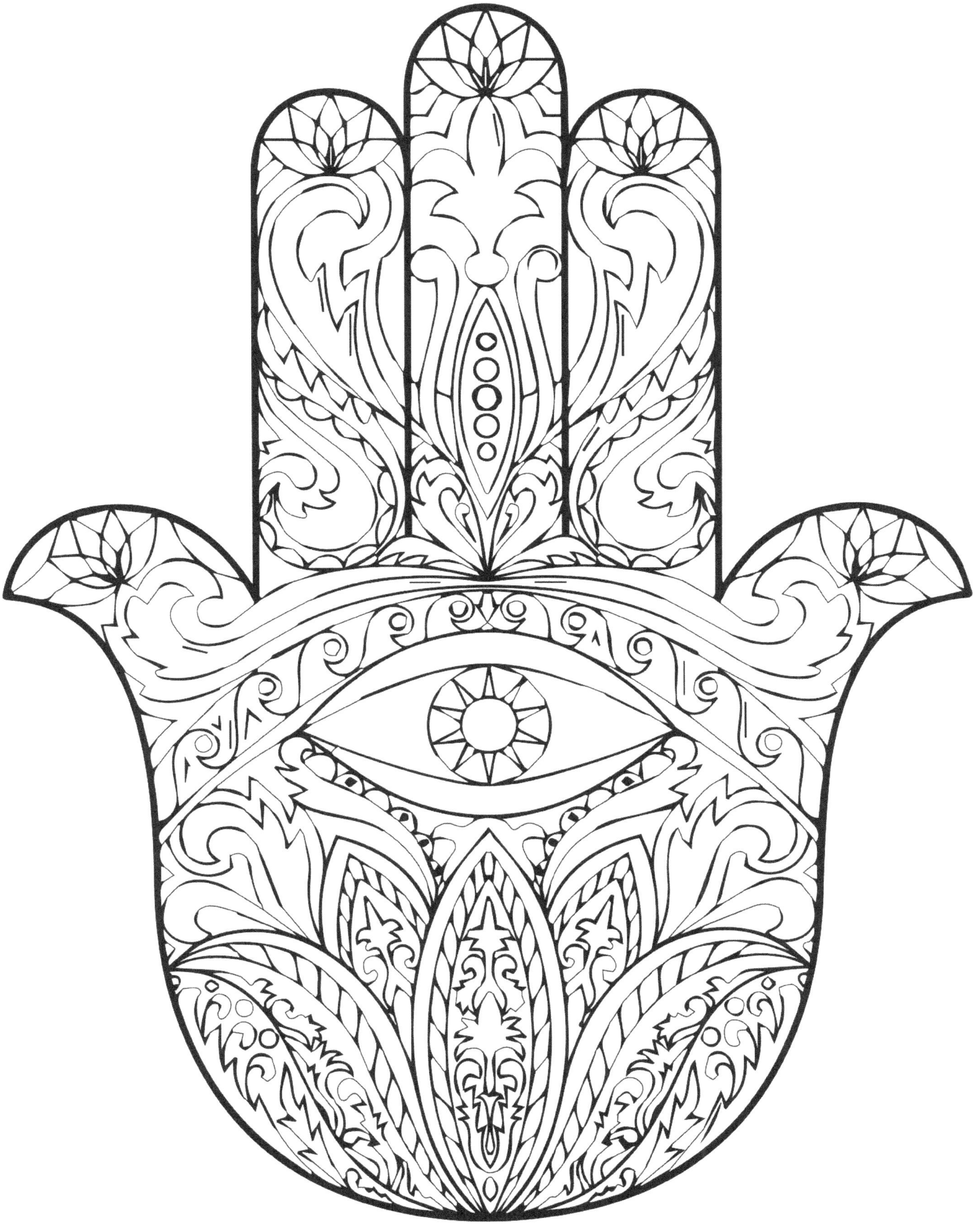

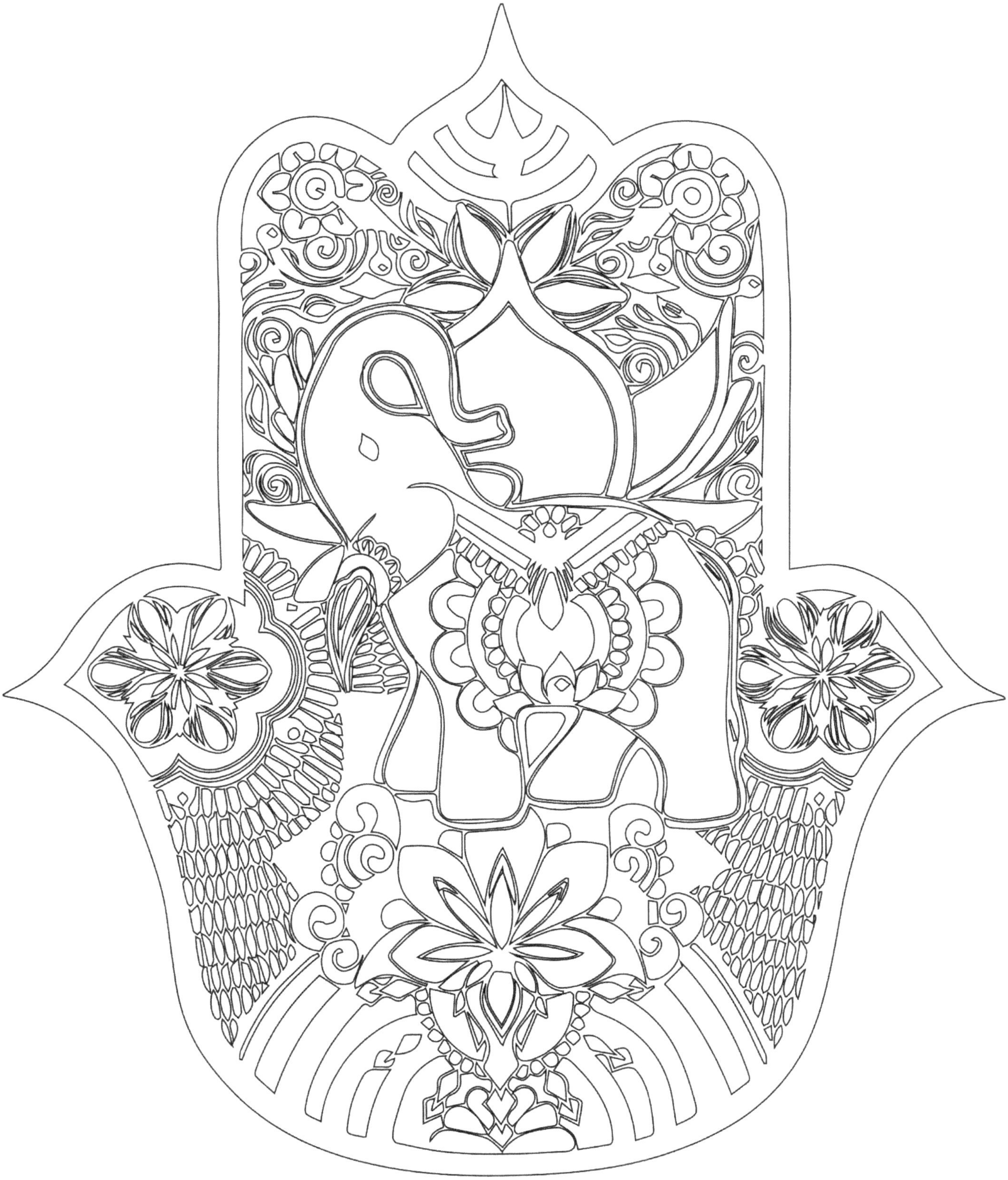

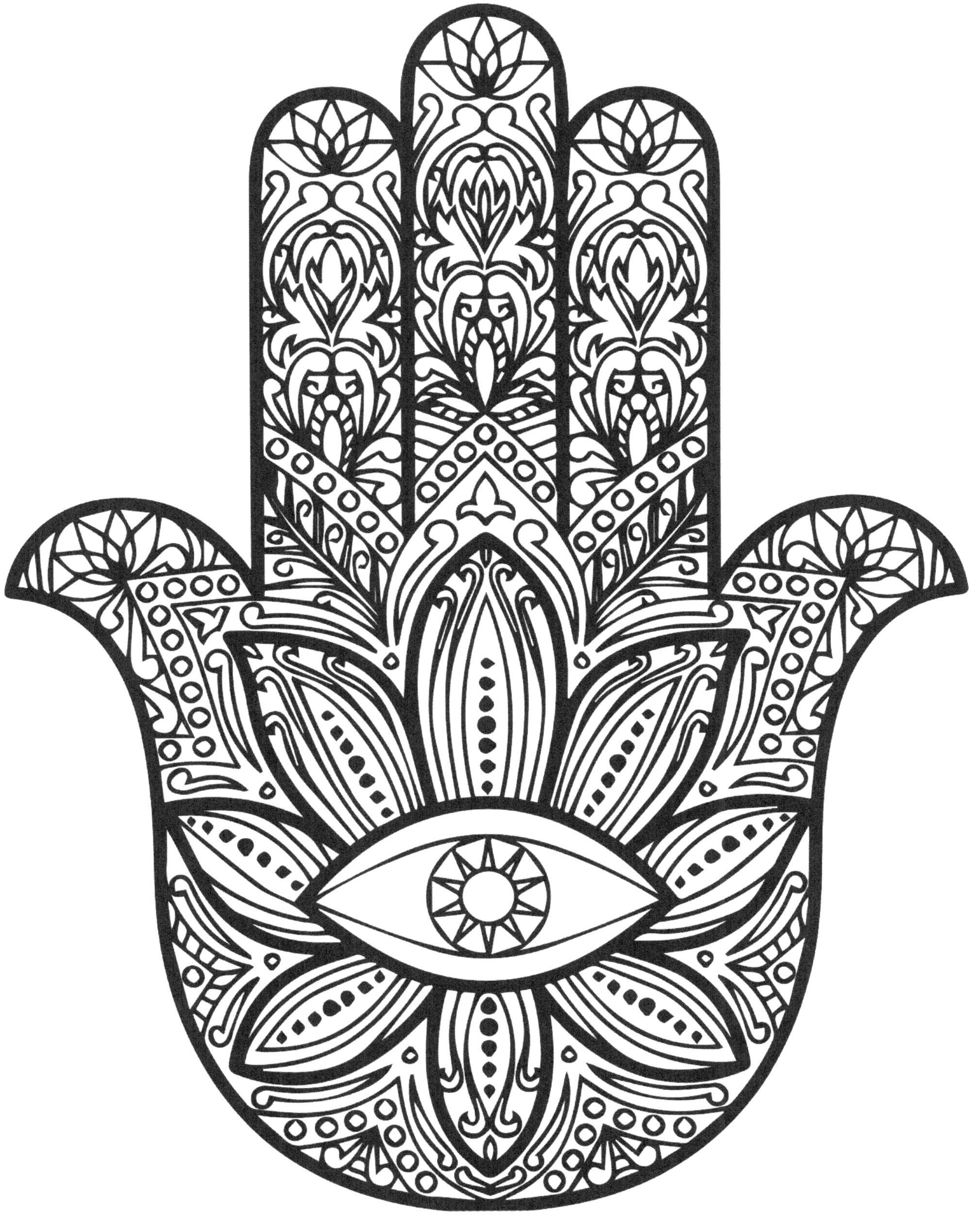

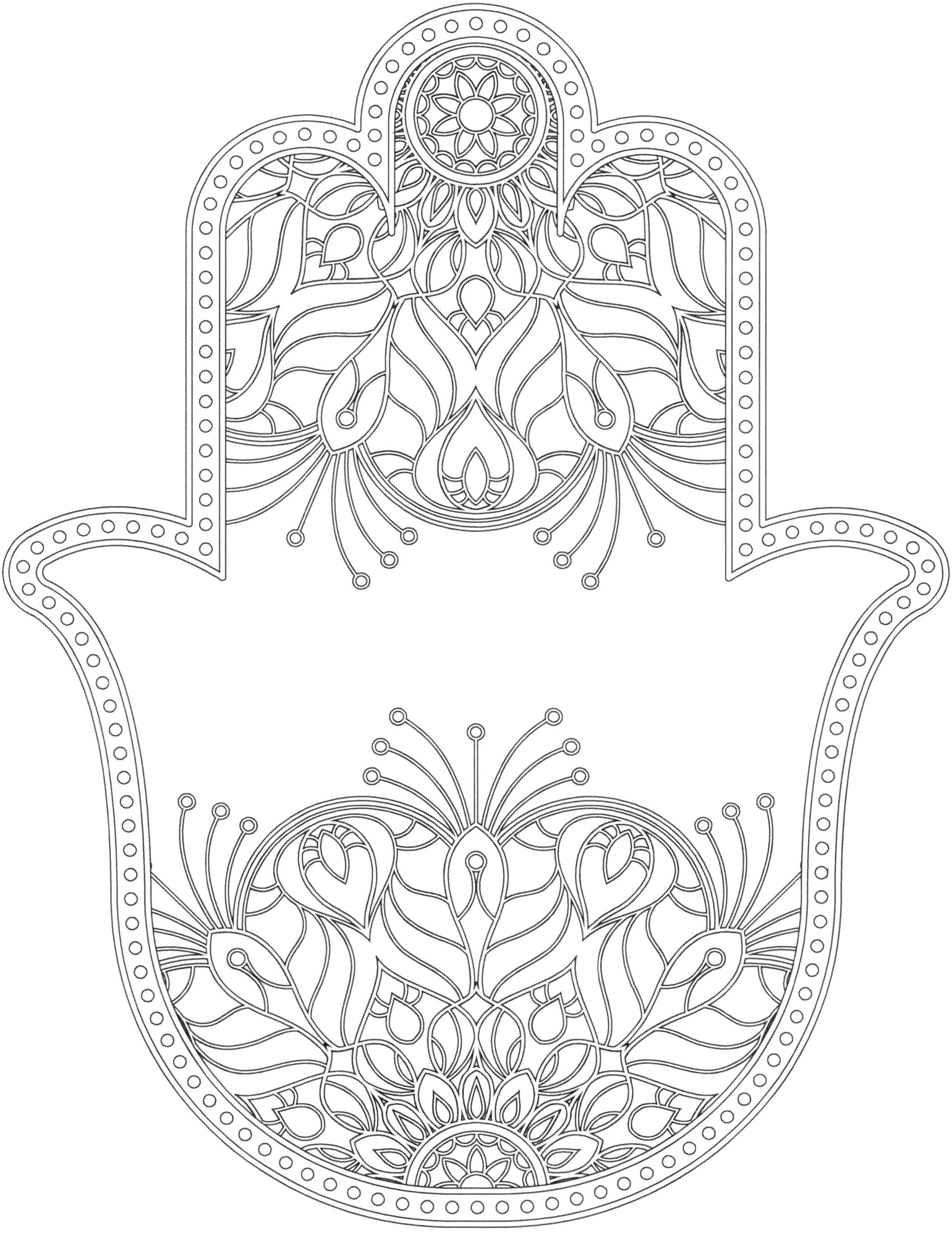

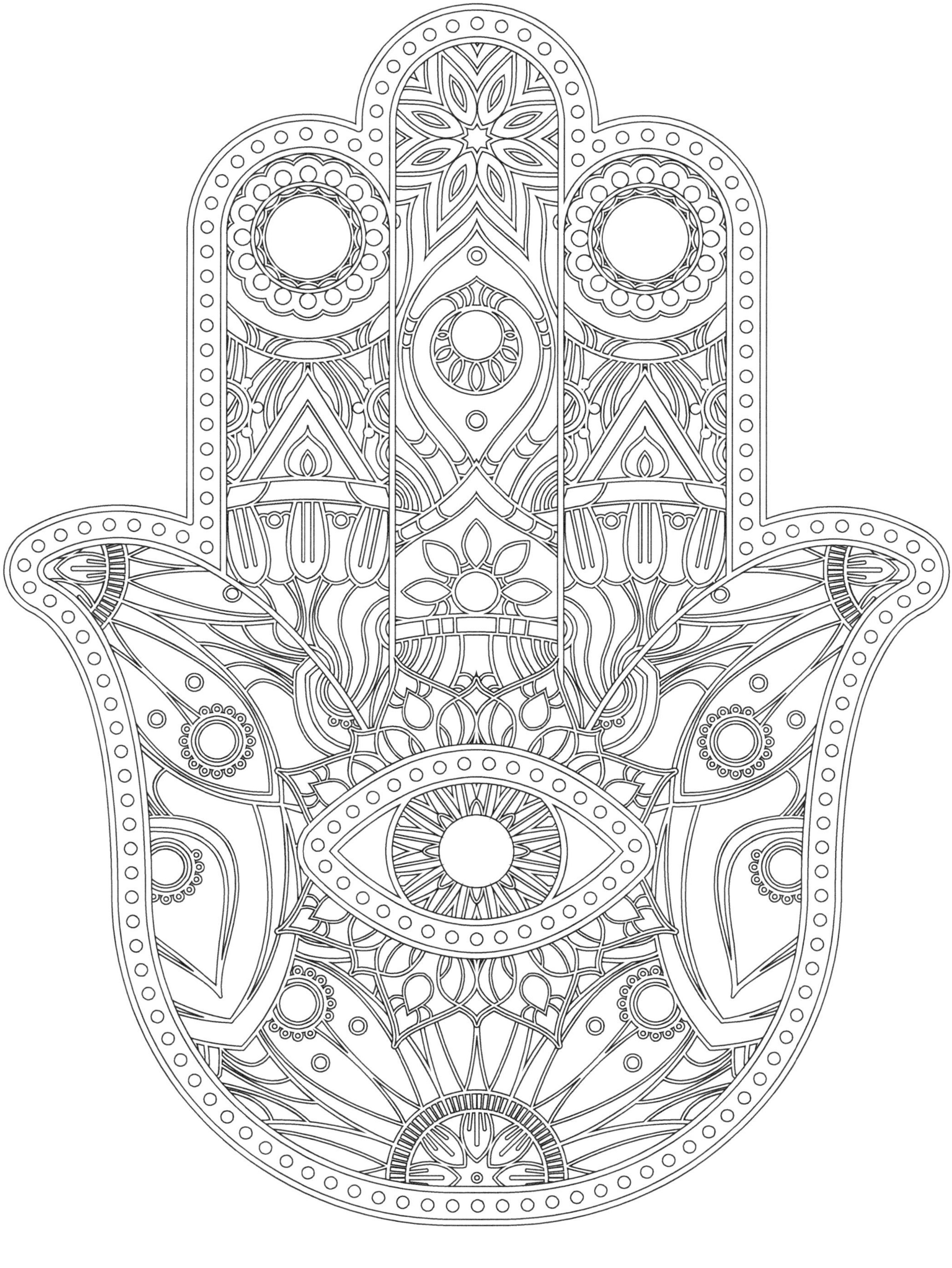

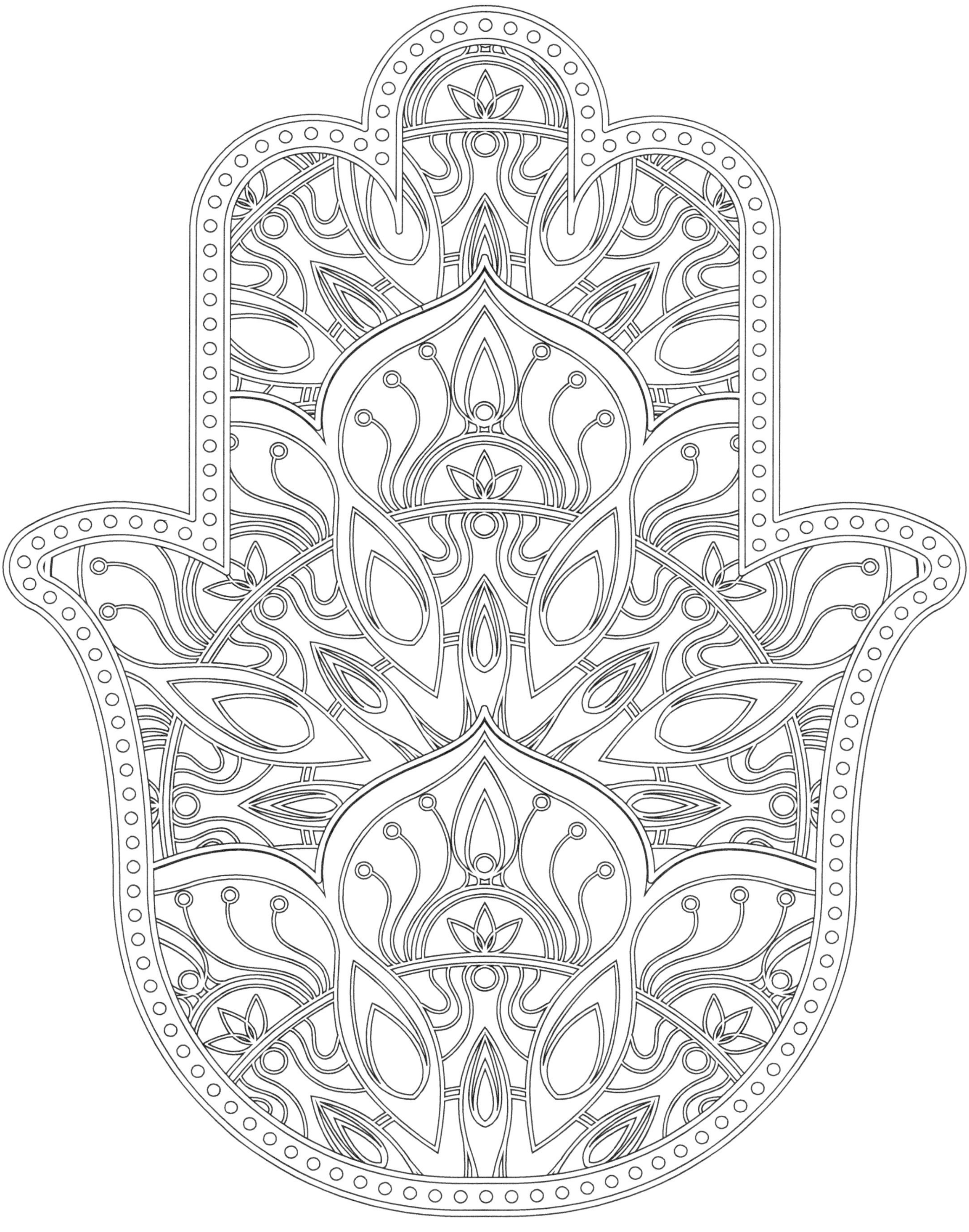

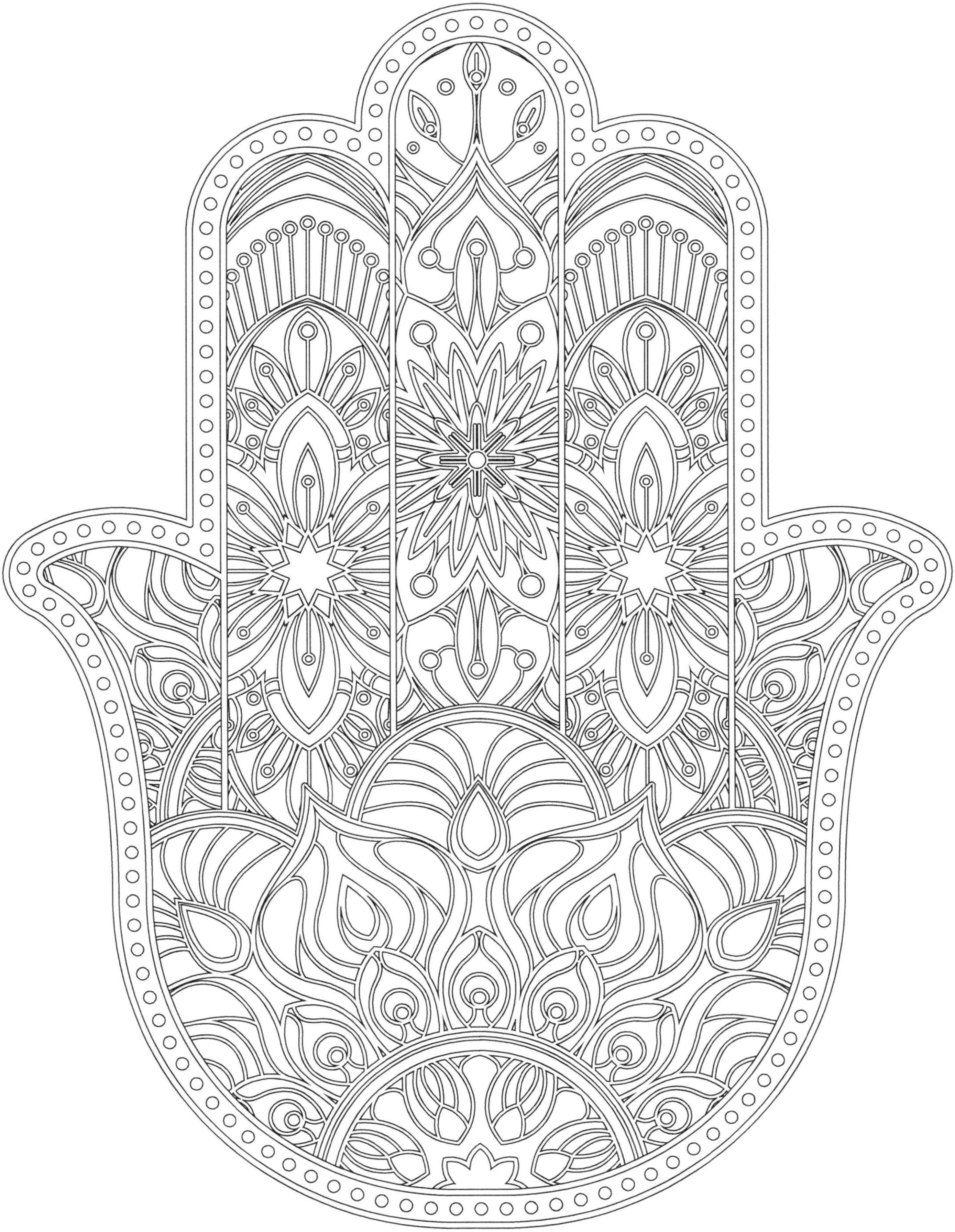

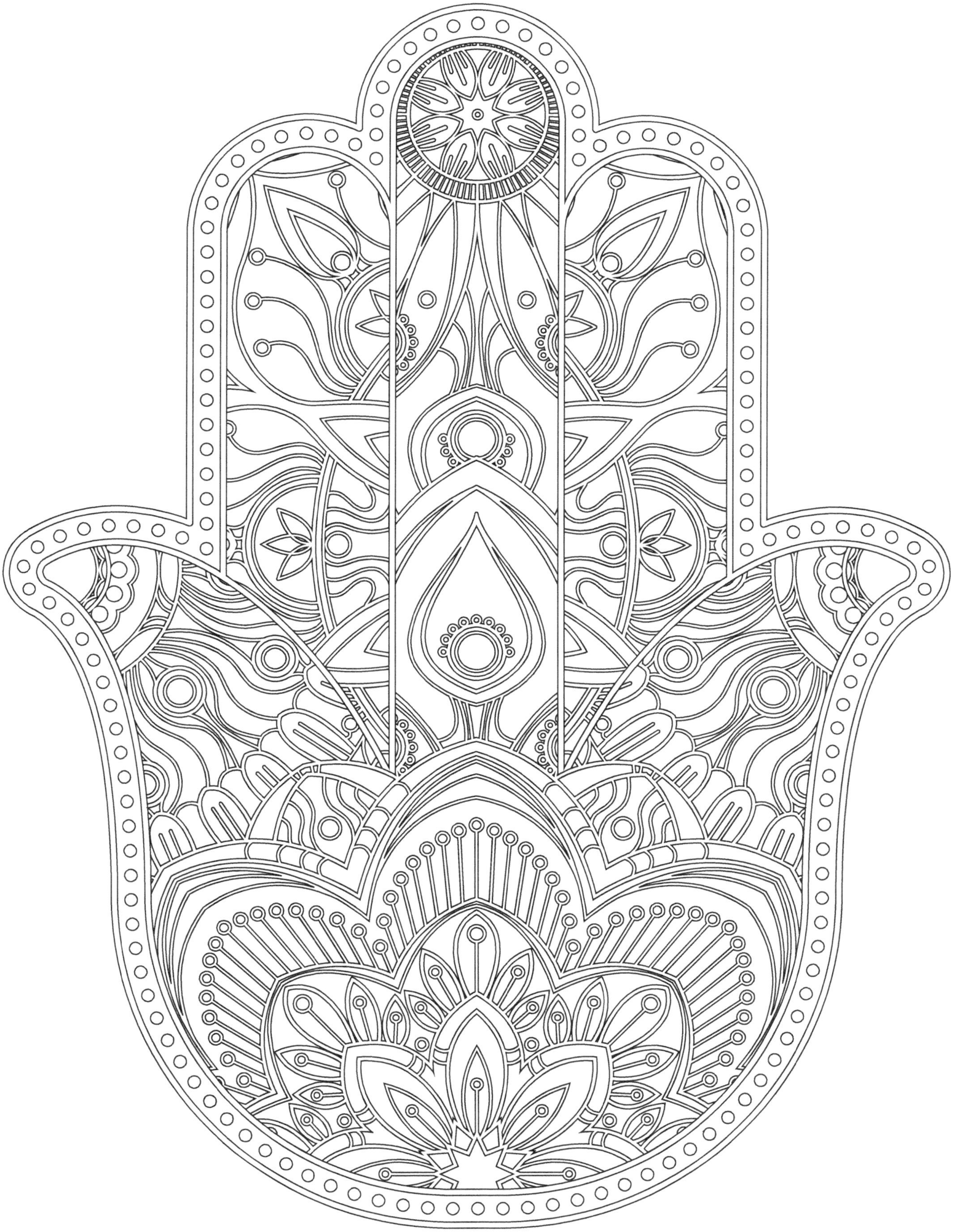

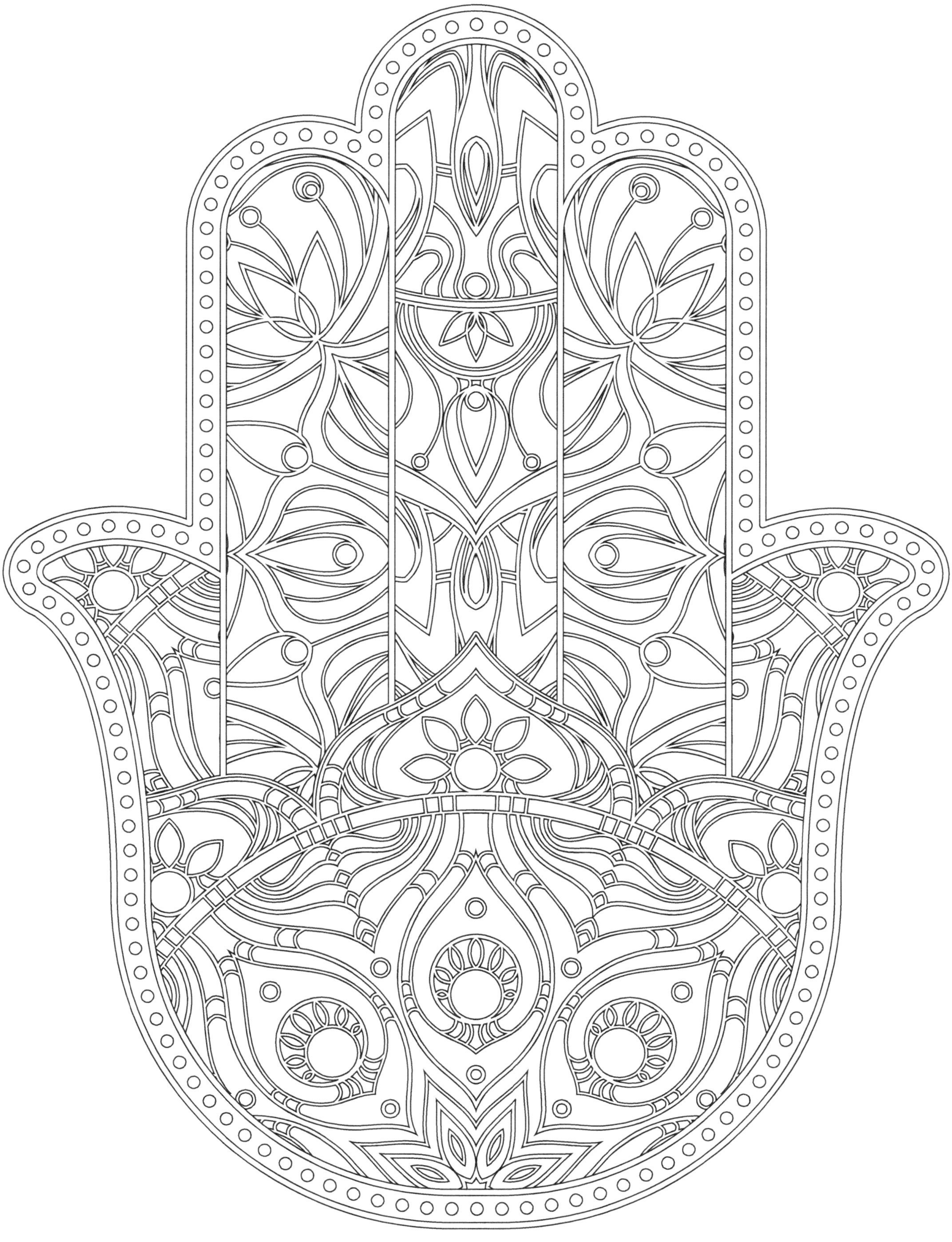

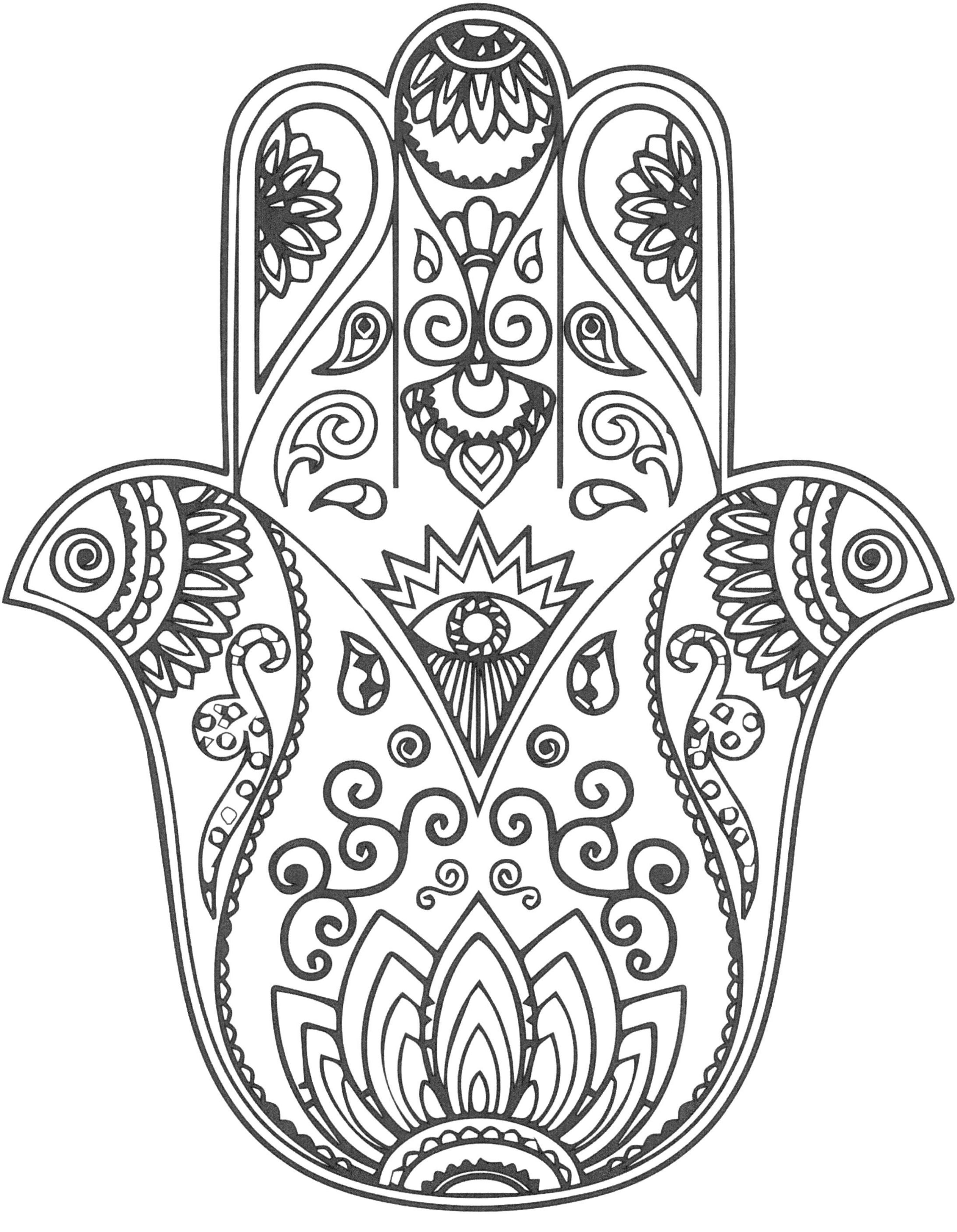

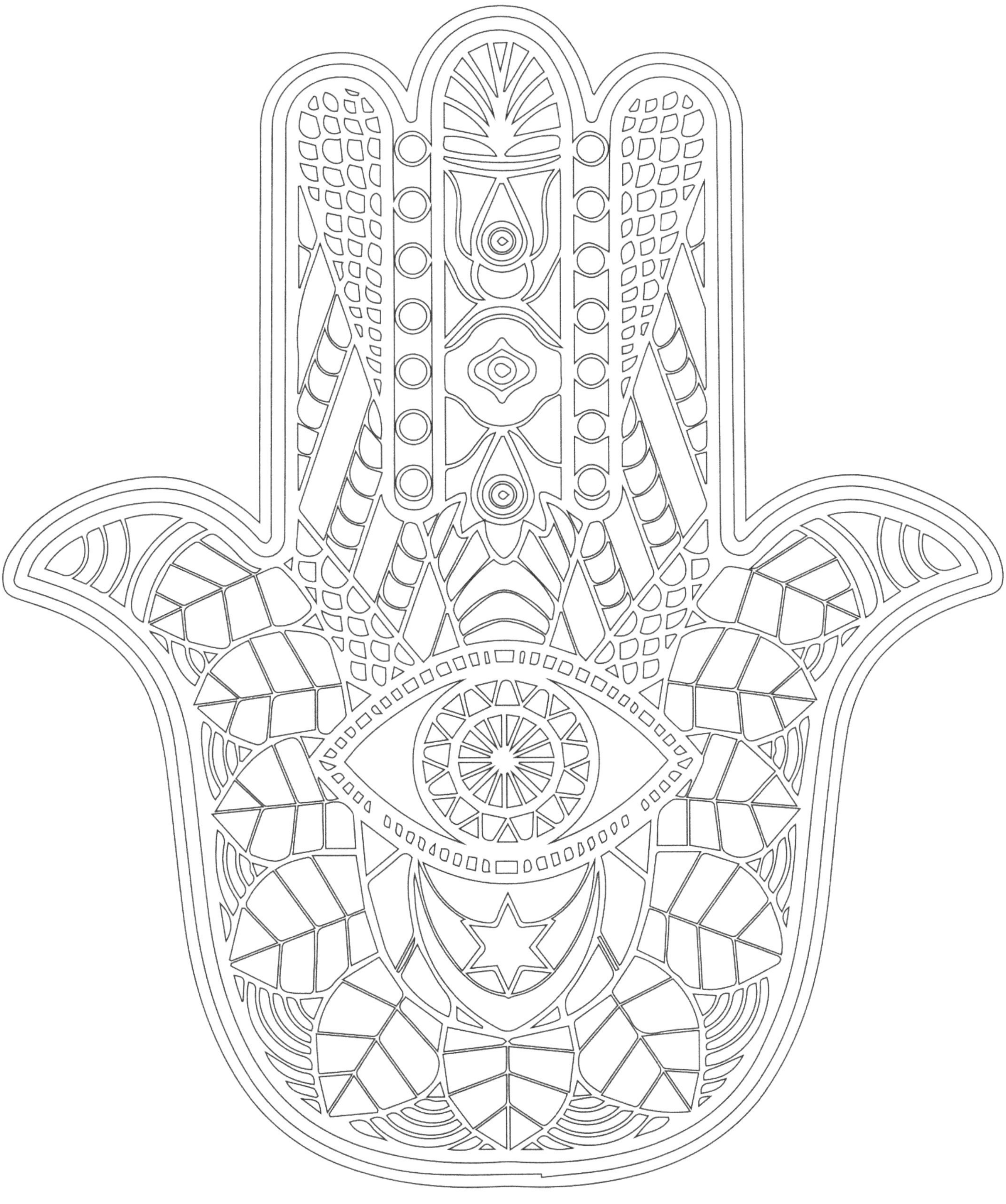

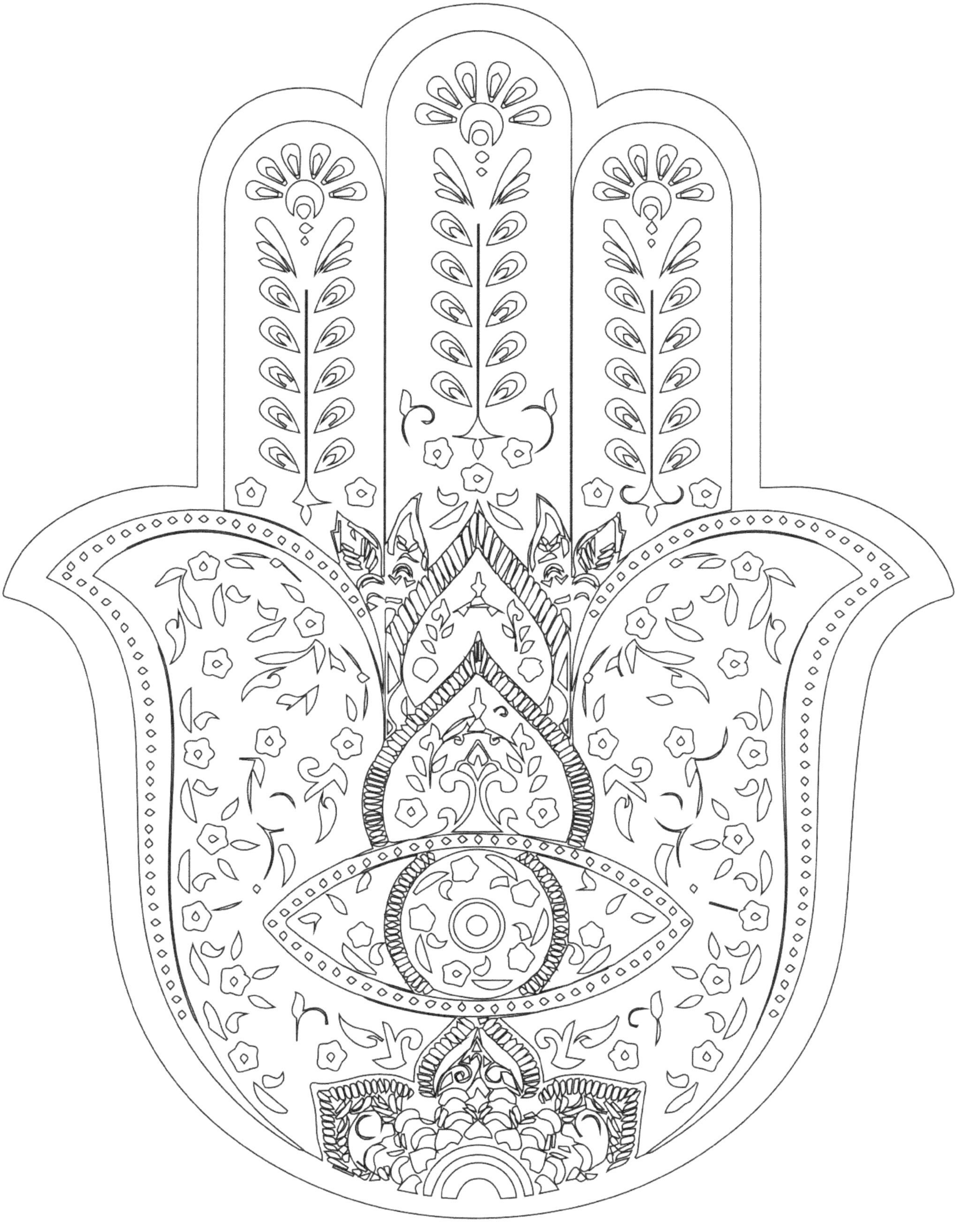

www.ingramcontent.com/pod-product-compliance
Lightning Source LLC
Chambersburg PA
CBHW080517220526
45465CB00006B/2509
* 9 7 9 8 6 4 6 1 1 3 2 9 1 *